G R A P H I S T — S H I R T   1

GRAPHIS T-SHIRT 1

....

An International Compilation of the Best in T-Shirt Design

Eine internationale Zusammenstellung des besten T-Shirt-Designs

An International Compilation of the Best in T-Shirt Design

Edited by · Herausgegeben von · Edité par:

B. Martin Pedersen

Publisher and Creative Director: B. Martin Pedersen

Editors: Annette Crandall, Heinke Jenssen

Art Directors: B. Martin Pedersen, Randell Pearson, Greg Simpson

Graphis Press Corp. Zürich (Switzerland)

(OPPOSITE PAGE) Art Director/Designer/Illustrator: JOHN SAYLES Photographer: JOHN CLARK Model: GINGER NICOL Design Firm/Client: SAYLES GRAPHIC DESIGN Country: USA ■ (NEXT PAGE) Art Director: BARRIE TUCKER Designer: BARRIE TUCKER Photographer: STEVE KEOUGH Model: BARRIE TUCKER Design Firm/Client: TUCKER DESIGN PTY LTD. Country: AUSTRALIA ■ BACKGROUND T-SHIRT IMAGE (THROUGHOUT) Photographer: DARRIN HADDAD

CONTENTS · INHALT · SOMMAIRE

REMARKS

WE EXTEND OUR HEARTFELT THANKS TO CONTRIBUTORS THROUGHOUT THE WORLD WHO HAVE MADE IT POSSIBLE TO PUBLISH A WIDE AND INTERNATIONAL SPECTRUM OF THE BEST WORK IN THIS FIELD.

ENTRY INSTRUCTIONS MAY BE REQUESTED AT:
GRAPHIS PRESS CORP.,
DUFOURSTRASSE 107,
8008 ZÜRICH, SWITZERLAND

ANMERKUNGEN

UNSER DANK GILT DEN EINSENDERN AUS ALLER WELT, DIE ES UNS DURCH IHRE BEI-TRÄGE ERMÖGLICHT HABEN, EIN BREITES, INTERNATIONALES SPEKTRUM DER BESTEN ARBEITEN ZU VERÖFFENTLICHEN.

TEILNAHMEBEDINGUNGEN:
GRAPHIS VERLAG AG,
DUFOURSTRASSE 107,
8008 ZÜRICH, SCHWEIZ

ANNOTATIONS

TOUTE NOTRE RECONNAISSANCE VA AUX DESIGNERS DU MONDE ENTIER DONT LES ENVOIS NOUS ONT PERMIS DE CONSTITUER UN VASTE PANORAMA INTERNATIONAL DES MEILLEURES CRÉATIONS.

MODALITÉS D'ENVOI DE TRAVAUX:
EDITIONS GRAPHIS,
DUFOURSTRASSE 107,
8008 ZÜRICH, SUISSE

GRAPHIS PUBLICATIONS

GRAPHIS, THE INTERNATIONAL BI-MONTHLY JOURNAL OF VISUAL COMMUNICATION
GRAPHIS DESIGN, THE INTERNATIONAL ANNUAL OF DESIGN AND ILLUSTRATION
GRAPHIS PHOTO, THE INTERNATIONAL ANNUAL OF PHOTOGRAPHY
GRAPHIS POSTER, THE INTERNATIONAL ANNUAL OF POSTER ART
GRAPHIS NUDES, A COLLECTION OF CAREFULLY SELECTED SOPHISTICATED IMAGES
GRAPHIS T-SHIRT, AN INTERNATIONAL COMPILATION OF THE BEST IN T-SHIRT DESIGN
GRAPHIS PACKAGING, AN INTERNATIONAL SURVEY OF PACKAGING DESIGN
GRAPHIS LETTERHEAD, AN INTERNATIONAL COMPILATION OF LETTERHEAD DESIGN
GRAPHIS DIAGRAM, THE GRAPHIC VISUALIZATION OF ABSTRACT, TECHNICAL AND STATISTICAL FACTS AND FUNCTIONS
GRAPHIS LOGO, AN INTERNATIONAL COMPILATION OF LOGOS
GRAPHIS PUBLICATION, AN INTERNATIONAL SURVEY OF THE BEST IN MAGAZINE DESIGN
GRAPHIS ANNUAL REPORTS, AN INTERNATIONAL COMPILATION OF THE BEST DESIGNED ANNUAL REPORTS
GRAPHIS CORPORATE IDENTITY, AN INTERNATIONAL COMPILATION OF THE BEST IN CORPORATE IDENTITY DESIGN
GRAPHIS TYPOGRAPHY, AN INTERNATIONAL COMPILATION OF OF THE BEST IN TYPOGRAPHIC DESIGN
ART FOR SURVIVAL: THE ILLUSTRATOR AND THE ENVIRONMENT, A DOCUMENT OF ART IN THE SERVICE OF MAN.
THE GRAPHIC DESIGNER'S GREEN BOOK, ENVIRONMENTAL RESOURCES FOR THE DESIGN AND PRINT INDUSTRIES

GRAPHIS PUBLIKATIONEN

GRAPHIS, DIE INTERNATIONALE ZWEIMONATSZEITSCHRIFT DER VISUELLEN KOMMUNIKATION
GRAPHIS DESIGN, DAS INTERNATIONALE JAHRBUCH ÜBER DESIGN UND ILLUSTRATION
GRAPHIS PHOTO, DAS INTERNATIONALE JAHRBUCH DER PHOTOGRAPHIE
GRAPHIS POSTER, DAS INTERNATIONALE JAHRBUCH DER PLAKATKUNST
GRAPHIS NUDES, EINE SAMMLUNG SORGFÄLTIG AUSGEWÄHLTER AKTPHOTOGRAPHIE
GRAPHIS T-SHIRT, EINE INTERNATIONALE ZUSAMMENSTELLUNG DES BESTEN T-SHIRT-DESIGNS
GRAPHIS PACKAGING, EIN INTERNATIONALER ÜBERBLICK ÜBER DIE PACKUNGSGESTALTUNG
GRAPHIS LETTERHEAD, EIN INTERNATIONALER ÜBERBLICK ÜBER BRIEFPAPIERGESTALTUNG
GRAPHIS DIAGRAM, DIE GRAPHISCHE DARSTELLUNG ABSTRAKTER TECHNISCHER UND STATISTISCHER DATEN UND FAKTEN
GRAPHIS LOGO, EINE INTERNATIONALE AUSWAHL VON FIRMEN-LOGOS
GRAPHIS MAGAZINDESIGN, EINE INTERNATIONALE ZUSAMMENSTELLUNG DES BESTEN ZEITSCHRIFTEN-DESIGNS
GRAPHIS ANNUAL REPORTS, EIN INTERNATIONALER ÜBERBLICK ÜBER DIE GESTALTUNG VON JAHRESBERICHTEN
GRAPHIS CORPORATE IDENTITY, EINE INTERNATIONALE AUSWAHL DES BESTEN CORPORATE IDENTITY DESIGNS
GRAPHIS TYPOGRAPHY, EINE INTERNATIONALE ZUSAMMENSTELLUNG DES BESTEN TYPOGRAPHIE DESIGN
ART FOR SURVIVAL: THE ILLUSTRATOR AND THE ENVIRONMENT, EIN DOKUMENT ÜBER DIE KUNST IM DIENSTE DES MENSCHEN
THE GRAPHIC DESIGNER'S GREEN BOOK, UMWELTKONZEPTE DER DESIGN- UND DRUCKINDUSTRIE

PUBLICATIONS GRAPHIS

GRAPHIS, LA REVUE BIMESTRIELLE INTERNATIONALE DE LA COMMUNICATION VISUELLE
GRAPHIS DESIGN, LE RÉPERTOIRE INTERNATIONAL DE LA COMMUNICATION VISUELLE
GRAPHIS PHOTO, LE RÉPERTOIRE INTERNATIONAL DE LA PHOTOGRAPHIE
GRAPHIS POSTER, LE RÉPERTOIRE INTERNATIONAL DE L'AFFICHE
GRAPHIS NUDES, UN FLORILEGE DE LA PHOTOGRAPHIE DE NUS
GRAPHIS T-SHIRT, AN INTERNATIONAL COMPILATION OF THE BEST IN T-SHIRT DESIGN
GRAPHIS PACKAGING, LE RÉPERTOIRE INTERNATIONAL DE LA CRÉATION D'EMBALLAGES
GRAPHIS LETTERHEAD, LE RÉPERTOIRE INTERNATIONAL DU DESIGN DE PAPIER À LETTRES
GRAPHIS DIAGRAM, LE RÉPERTOIRE GRAPHIQUE DE FAITS ET DONNÉES ABSTRAITS, TECHNIQUES ET STATISTIQUES
GRAPHIS LOGO, LE RÉPERTOIRE INTERNATIONAL DU LOGO
GRAPHIS PUBLICATION, LE RÉPERTOIRE INTERNATIONAL DU DESIGN DE PÉRIODIQUES
GRAPHIS ANNUAL REPORTS, PANORAMA INTERNATIONAL DU MEILLEUR DESIGN DE RAPPORTS ANNUELS D'ENTREPRISES
GRAPHIS CORPORATE IDENTITY, PANORAMA INTERNATIONAL DU MEILLEUR DESIGN D'IDENTITÉ CORPORATE
GRAPHIS TYPOGRAPHY, LE RÉPERTOIRE INTERNATIONAL DU MEILLEUR DESIGN DE TYPOGRAPHIE
ART FOR SURVIVAL: THE ILLUSTRATOR AND THE ENVIRONMENT, L'ART AU SERVICE DE LA SURVIE
THE GRAPHIC DESIGNER'S GREEN BOOK, L'ÉCOLOGIE APPLIQUÉE AU DESIGN ET À L'INDUSTRIE GRAPHIQUE

PUBLICATION NO. 228 (ISBN 3-85709-444.3)
© COPYRIGHT UNDER UNIVERSAL COPYRIGHT CONVENTION
COPYRIGHT © 1994 BY GRAPHIS PRESS CORP., DUFOURSTRASSE 107, 8008 ZURICH, SWITZERLAND
JACKET AND BOOK DESIGN COPYRIGHT © 1994 BY PEDERSEN DESIGN
141 LEXINGTON AVENUE, NEW YORK, N.Y. 10016 USA

PRINTED IN JAPAN BY TOPPAN PRINTING CO., LTD.

COMMENTARY

KOMMENTAR

COMMENTAIRE

Paul Kalkbrenner

The printed T-shirt is one of the few media that have successfully resisted monopolization. True, big companies use T-shirts to promote their corporate identities. And by the 1970s the music business and its megastars had discovered that merchandising can be at least as profitable as music. But fortunately, the medium is such an unlimited pool of new ideas that the big merchandisers have trouble keeping up with what's currently hip with the kids. In the arena of heavy metal with its overused skull imagery nothing new has happened in years, while in another camp people still can think of nothing better than printing Madonna's face on T-shirts. Sure, dumb fans will buy anything, if only to prove that they have been at a legendary concert. But sometimes it is the stars themselves that defy market rules and come on stage in T-shirts that some guy has designed in his basement. Axl Rose, for one, turned such an underground design into a bestseller. It showed a woodcut of Jesus with the caption, "Kill Your Idols!" □ Artists have always favored silk-screening as a low-cost reproduction method. And in an era where almost everyone owns a PC or a Mac, everything, including distribution, has become much simpler. Sampling is being translated from the field of music to that of images and signs while the simulated worlds of advertising and the media are redefined through home computing. Under the gifted hands of rave artists, icons of Socialist Realism as well as ordinary chocolate package designs mutate into club wear for the techno scene. The hallowed copyright is shaking. □ A purist like Warhol faithfully copied his soup cans. Today, Nutella turns into Shootella and Toys 'r Us begets Beuys 'r Us. The scene disrespectfully quotes itself; countless versions of Smiley keep cropping up; graffiti as well as the blackmail-letter aesthetics of the Sex Pistols are being recycled on T-shirts; Australian designers borrow their images from aboriginal mythology. The boundaries between underground design and high fashion are dissolving. T-shirt and sportswear designs have propelled amateurs such as Stüssy into couture heaven. The skateboard and surfing subcultures have become a hotbed for fashion trends that are spearheaded by T-shirt designs. □ What remains the T-shirt's very own domain is its responsiveness to cultural and political trends. Nothing provokes better than a T-shirt, as many logo bootleggers find out when their designs suddenly draw legal attention. The powers that be thus underline their chronic lack of humor but also their ultimate impotence: once banned, a T-shirt reaches instant cult status and demand skyrockets. □ Ironically, that's the way my own T-shirt business got started. We took the anti-drug campaign of Germany's Federal Health Department (Keine Macht den Drogen/No Power to Drugs) and turned it into a send-up of stupidity, racism and xenophobia. A short time later, the advertising agency of the Health Department slapped us with a 500,000-mark suit. The media took our side and athletes, artists and popular musicians like Boy George supported us. Our T-shirt design spawned two CDs, a TV spot and a comedy show that shared the title of our T-shirt campaign, Keine Macht den Doofen (No Power to Dorks). The case was ultimately dismissed. We were merely ordered to change the color of the T-shirt but were allowed to continue production. The entire country was laughing about this legal farce. □ It is nice that the T-shirt of an Indie rock band can thus become a mass-produced item. But that wouldn't do for many club T-shirts or artist designs. They are produced in limited editions and serve as a medium for endlessly new ideas. Deliberately exclusive, they emphasize the individuality of the person wearing them. They also provide an opening line for many club kids: "Where did you get that T-shirt?" □ In both cases, one essential aspect of the medium becomes apparent: T-shirts foster communication. Unlike other media they prompt a direct exchange between people, not between a person and printed paper or between a screen and a couch potato. In times of rampant speechlessness a T-shirt sends an immediate signal between people. It may provoke a wink, shock or attraction. It initiates something—ideally that something would be contact between two people. ■

PAUL KALKBRENNER WAS BORN IN COLOGNE, GERMANY. AFTER AN APPRENTICESHIP AS A TYPESETTER HE STUDIED VISUAL COMMUNICATIONS. IN 1982 HE OPENED HIS OWN GRAPHIC DESIGN STUDIO AND ALSO WORKED AS A PHOTOGRAPHER AND ARTIST. AS OF 1987 HE WORKED AS PHOTOGRAPHER FOR SEVERAL MAGAZINES AND IN ADVERTISING. IN 1992 HE FOUNDED HIS PUBLISHING COMPANY, ABGANG!, WHICH DEALS MAINLY WITH T-SHIRTS, POSTCARDS AND MERCHANDISING. KALKBRENNER'S INTERESTS ALSO INCLUDE COMPUTER-AIDED DESIGN AND PHOTOGRAPHY.

Das bedruckte T-Shirt ist eines der wenigen Medien, dem es immer noch gelingt, sich der Monopolisierung zu entziehen. Sicher, grosse Konzerne nutzen es, um ihre Corporate Identity zu promoten, das Musikbusiness mit seinen Megastars hat spätestens seit den 70ern entdeckt, dass mit Merchandising oft mehr Geld zu verdienen ist als mit der Musik selbst. Leider – oder zum Glück – ist das Genre T-Shirt jedoch ein solch uferloser Pool von immer wieder neuen Ideen, dass es den grossen Merchandisern schwerfällt, mit dem Feeling der Kids Schritt zu halten. Im Bereich Heavy Metal, mit seinen sattsam bekannten Totenkopf-Designs, tut sich seit Jahren nichts Neues, ganz zu schweigen von jenen, denen nichts Besseres einfällt, als Madonnas Konterfei auf ein T-Shirt zu drucken. Sicher, der dumme Fan kauft alles und sei es nur, um zu beweisen, dass er bei einem legendären Konzert dabei war. Aber manchmal sind es die Stars selbst, die aus den Regeln des Marktes ausbrechen und sich auf der Bühne T-Shirts anziehen, die irgendein Freak in irgendeinem Hinterhof selbst gedruckt hat. Axl Rose (Guns 'n Roses) z.B. machte so aus einem Underground Shirt einen Bestseller. Darauf sah man einen Holzschnitt von Jesus Christus mit der Headline: Kill your Idols! ◻ Siebdruck war schon immer ein beliebtes Multiplikations-Verfahren bei Künstlern, weil es dabei keiner grossen Investitionen bedarf. Und in einem Zeitalter, wo fast jeder zu Hause seinen Amiga, Mac oder Dos stehen hat, ist alles, inklusive der Distribution, noch viel einfacher geworden. Samplingtechniken aus der Musik werden auf Bilder und Zeichen übertragen und die Simulationswelten der Werbung und der Medien per homecomputing und homeprinting neu definiert. Embleme des sozialistischen Realismus, ebenso wie ordinäre Schokoriegel-Designs mutieren unter den begabten Fingern von DTP-Freaks zu Club-Wear Shirts der Techno-Szene. Das geheiligte Copyright wankt. ◻ Während Warhol seine Suppendosen als Purist noch beliess wie das Original, wird heute aus Nutella Shootella, Toys 'r Us stand Pate für Beuys 'r Us. Und, die Szene zitiert respektlos sich selbst, unzählige Smiley Variationen erblicken noch immer das Licht der Welt, Graffitis werden ebenso auf T-Shirts recycelt wie die Erpresserbrief-Ästhetik der Sex Pistols. Australische Designer entleihen ihre Motive den Mythenwelten der Aborigines. Die Grenzen zur Mode sind fliessend. Ehemalige Non-Profis wie Stüssy dringen über T-Shirt- und Sportsweardesign in den Modeolymp vor. Aus Skate- und Surfboard-Clubs entwickeln sich Modetrends, deren Ursprung meist beim Medium T-Shirt zu finden ist. ◻ Doch eine ganz spezielle Domäne des T-Shirts bleibt die schnelle Reaktion auf kulturelle und politische Trends. Nichts provoziert besser als ein T-Shirt, und viele Insignia Hijacker machen denn auch als erstes Bekanntschaft mit Staats- und Rechtsanwälten. So lernen sie zwar einerseits die penetrante Humorlosigkeit der Mächtigen kennen, aber auch bisweilen deren Ohnmacht. T-Shirts, einmal verboten, erreichen sofort Kultstatus. Die Nachfrage steigt gewaltig. ◻ So entstand ironischerweise auch mein eigenes T-Shirt-Business. Aus der offiziellen Anti-Drogen-Kampagne des deutschen Bundesgesundheitsministeriums sampelten wir eine Parodie auf Dummheit, Zensur und Ausländerfeindlichkeit. Kurze Zeit später schneite uns eine 500 000-DM-Klage der Werbeagentur des Ministeriums ins Haus. Presse, Funk und Fernsehen stellten sich auf unsere Seite. Bekannte Musiker wie Boy George, Sportler und Künstler solidarisierten sich mit uns. Aus unserer T-Shirt Idee entstanden gleich zwei CDs, ein Fernsehspot und ein Kabarettprogramm gleichen Titels: Keine Macht den Doofen. Die Klage schliesslich scheiterte vor Gericht kläglich. Wir mussten lediglich die Farbe des T-Shirts ändern und durften weiter produzieren. Ganz Deutschland lachte über diese Justizposse. ◻ Schön, dass auf solche Art und Weise das T-Shirt einer Independent Rock Band plötzlich Massenware wird. Ganz im Gegensatz dazu verhält es sich mit vielen Dancefloor-Designs oder Künstler T-Shirts. Bewusst werden kleine Auflagen produziert und immer wieder neue Ideen realisiert. Hier zählt die Exklusivität, die nicht zuletzt den Träger als etwas Besonderes ausweisen. So beginnt denn in vielen Clubs bisweilen das Gespräch mit «Wo hast du dieses T-Shirt her?» ◻ In beiden Fällen zeigt sich ein wesentlicher Aspekt der Ware T-Shirt: Der Kommunikationsfaktor. Anders als bei anderen Medien wird nämlich Kommunikation zwischen leibhaftigen Menschen provoziert und nicht etwa, wie bei Zeitschriften, zwischen bedrucktem Papier und Mensch oder zwischen Bildschirm und lethargischem Konsument. In Zeiten allgemeiner Sprachlosigkeit setzt ein T-Shirt direkt ein Signal zwischen Menschen. Provoziert es ein Augenzwinkern, Schock oder Sympathie. Aber es bewegt etwas – im besten Falle zwei Menschen aufeinander zu. ∎

PAUL KALKBRENNER, IN KÖLN GEBOREN, MACHTE EINE SCHRIFTSETZERLEHRE, BEVOR ER VISUELLE KOMMUNIKATION AN DER FH KÖLN STUDIERTE. 1982 GRÜNDETE ER EIN EIGENES GRAPHIK-DESIGN STUDIO UND BETÄTIGTE SICH AUCH ALS PHOTOGRAPH UND FREIER KÜNSTLER. SEIT 1980 GAB ES AUSSTELLUNGEN SEINER PHOTOGRAPHIE UND INSTALLATIONEN IN VERSCHIEDENEN GROSSSTÄDTEN. AB 1987 ARBEITETE ER AUCH ALS PHOTOGRAPH FÜR VERSCHIEDENE ZEITSCHRIFTEN UND IN DER WERBUNG. DER SCHWERPUNKT WAREN PORTRÄTS VON KÜNSTLERN UND MUSIKERN. 1992 GRÜNDETE ER DEN VERLAG ABGANG, DER SICH VOR ALLEM MIT T-SHIRTS POSTKARTEN UND MERCHANDISING BEFASST. SEIT 1993 BESCHÄFTIGT ER SICH AUCH MIT COMPUTERAIDED DESIGN UND PHOTOGRAPHIE.

Le T-shirt imprimé est l'un des rares supports qui réussisse encore à échapper au monopole. Bien sûr, d'importants groupes l'utilisent pour promouvoir leur identité visuelle. Dans les années 70, l'industrie du disque avec ses mégastars découvrait que le merchandising est souvent plus lucratif que la musique elle-même. Hélas – ou heureusement! – le T-shirt semble être une source inépuisable de créativité, capable de suivre le rythme de la jeunesse. Dans le domaine du «heavy metal», identifiable par ses célèbres motifs têtes de mort, il n'est rien d'innovant depuis des années. Sans parler des esprits dénués d'imagination dont les créations se limitent aux T-shirts à l'effigie de Madonna. Bien sûr, le fan de base achète tout, sans discernement, ne serait-ce que pour montrer qu'il a assisté à un concert légendaire. Mais il arrive aussi que les stars elles-mêmes échappent aux règles du marché et apparaissent sur scène vêtues d'un T-shirt qu'un illustre inconnu a imprimé dans un fond de cour. Axl Rose du groupe Guns'n Roses, par exemple, fit un bestseller d'un T-shirt «underground». Motif de l'engouement: Jésus Christ, accompagné du slogan «Kill your idols»! (Tue tes idols!) □ La sérigraphie était déjà un procédé de reproduction cher aux artistes car elle n'exige pas de gros investissements. A une époque où chaque foyer possède son Amiga, son Mac ou son Dos, tout est devenu beaucoup plus facile, y compris la distribution. Les techniques de sampling empruntées à la musique ont été appliquées aux photos et aux dessins. Les ordinateurs et imprimantes personnels ont redéfini les univers de la simulation, ces outils privilégiés de la publicité et des médias. Les emblèmes du réalisme socialiste, tout comme les vulgaires motifs de barres de chocolat, se muent en T-shirts techno sous les doigts agiles de fanas d'images de synthèse. Coup dur pour les droits d'auteurs! □ Alors que Warhol, en puriste, n'a pas trahi ses modèles en peignant ses boîtes de soupe, Nutella se transforme de nos jours en Shootella, Beuys'r Us s'inspire de Toys'r Us. Les graffitis connaissent une nouvelle existence sur les T-shirts et les créateurs australiens empruntent leurs motifs aux mythes des Aborigènes. Les frontières de la mode sont bien floues. D'anciens amateurs se sont hissés au sommet de l'Olympe de la mode en créant des T-shirts et des articles de sportwear. Les nouvelles tendances de la mode sont souvent nées sur des T-shirts, dans des clubs de planches à roulettes ou de surf. □ Réagir rapidement aux mouvements et mouvances culturels et politiques est en effet une spécialité du T-shirt. Rien ne provoque mieux qu'un T-shirt et nombreux sont les pirates du graphisme textile ayant eu affaire à la justice. Il est vrai qu'ils font ainsi l'apprentissage de la sévérité pénétrante des hommes de pouvoir, mais aussi, éventuellement, de leur impuissance. Les T-shirts condamnés sont aussitôt élevés au rang d'objets cultes, la demande augmentant alors considérablement. □ L'ironie du sort voulut que ma propre affaire de T-shirts connut des prémices similaires. Inspirés par la campagne antidrogue du ministère de la santé allemand, nous avions concocté une parodie de la bêtise, de la censure et de la xénophobie. Peu de temps après, l'agence de publicité du ministère portait plainte et nous réclamait 500 000 DM de dommages et intérêts. La presse, la radio et la télévision prirent notre défense. Des chanteurs connus, des sportifs et des artistes nous apportèrent leur soutien. Tant et si bien que l'idée de départ du T-shirt donna lieu à l'enregistrement de deux CD, d'un spot TV, et à un programme de café-théâtre portant le même titre: Keine Macht den Doofen (Pas de pouvoir aux imbéciles). La plainte fut lamentablement rejetée. Nous fûmes simplement contraints de modifier la couleur du T-shirt, et la production put se poursuivre. L'Allemagne entière fit des gorges chaudes de cette farce juridique. □ Tant mieux si le T-shirt d'un groupe de rock peut devenir soudainement un produit de masse. Il en est tout autrement des T-shirts de clubs ou d'artistes. Ces derniers sont intentionnellement imprimés en nombre limité et leurs motifs, constamment renouvelés. Pour ce type de produit, il n'est que l'exclusivité qui compte, puisqu'il est sensé donner une touche toute particulière à la personne qui le porte. Et dans les clubs, il n'est pas rare que la conversation s'engage ainsi: «Dis-moi, où as-tu trouvé ce T-shirt?» □ Ces deux cas de figure révèlent un aspect remarquable du produit T-shirt: le facteur communication. En effet, ce support original permet d'établir directement le contact entre deux êtres humains, sans passer, comme les autres médias, par l'imprimé ou l'écran du consommateur léthargique. Dans un monde souffrant d'incommunicabilité chronique, le T-shirt établit le contact entre les hommes. Qu'il déclenche un simple clin d'œil, qu'il choque ou attire la sympathie, il fait bouger les choses... et dans le meilleur des cas, il rapproche les hommes. ■

PAUL KALKBRENNER EST NÉ À COLOGNE, OÙ IL A FAIT UN APPRENTISSAGE DE TYPOGRAPHE AVANT D'ÉTUDIER LA COMMUNICATION VISUELLE. EN 1982, IL OUVRE SON PROPRE ATELIER DE CRÉATION GRAPHIQUE, TOUT EN SE CONSACRANT À L'ART ET À LA PHOTOGRAPHIE. DEPUIS 1980, SES ŒUVRES PHOTOGRAPHIQUES ONT ÉTÉ PRÉSENTÉES DANS PLUSIEURS GRANDES VILLES. DÈS 1987, IL TRAVAILLE ÉGALEMENT COMME PHOTOGRAPHE POUR DIVERS MAGAZINES ET POUR LA PUBLICITÉ, EN SE SPÉCIALISANT DANS LES PORTRAITS D'ARTISTES ET DE MUSICIENS. EN 1992, IL CRÉE LA SOCIÉTÉ ABGANG!, QUI VEND DES T-SHIRTS, DES CARTES POSTALES ET DES ARTICLES DE MERCHANDISING. DEPUIS 1993, KALKBRENNER S'INTÉRESSE ÉGALEMENT À LA PHOTOGRAPHIE ET AU DESSIN ASSISTÉ PAR ORDINATEUR.

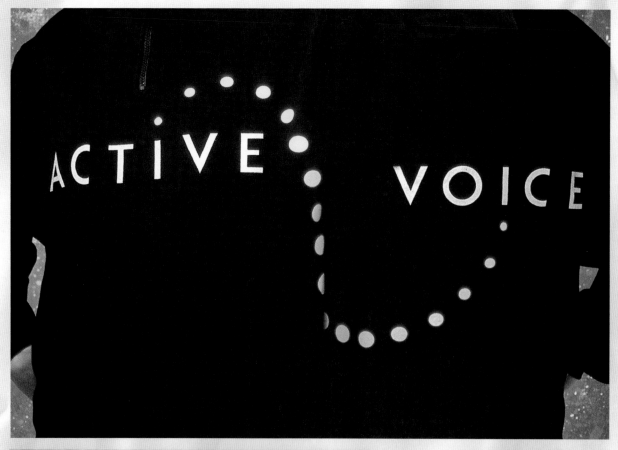

(PRECEEDING SPREAD) ■ 1 ART DIRECTOR: JACK ANDERSON DESIGNERS: JACK ANDERSON, JULIA LAPINE, DAVID BATES DESIGN FIRM: HORNALL ANDERSON DESIGN WORKS CLIENT: ACTIVE VOICE COUNTRY: USA ■ 2 ART DIRECTOR: ALISON TOMLIN DESIGNER: ALISON TOMLIN ILLUSTRATOR: ALISON TOMLIN DESIGN FIRM: CARTER WONG LTD. CLIENT: QUASAR COUNTRY: GREAT BRITAIN ■ 3 ART DIRECTOR: AXEL SCHMALSCHLÄGER DESIGNERS: MARKUS SCHMIDT, RICHARD SCHWEIGER ILLUSTRATORS: MARKUS SCHMIDT, RICHARD SCHWEIGER PHOTOGRAPHER:

CHRISTOFER TECH DESIGN FIRM: STAWICKI WERBEAGENTUR CLIENT: WYSE TECHNOLOGY COUNTRY: GERMANY ■
(THIS SPREAD, LEFT) ART DIRECTOR: BERNHARD H. TINZ DESIGNER: CAROLINE FEIGENSPAN PHOTOGRAPHER: RH
STUDIO WERBEPHOTOGRAPHIE DESIGN FIRM: TINZ DCC CLIENT: M. KAINDL HOLZINDUSTRIE COUNTRY: AUSTRIA ■
(THIS SPREAD, RIGHT) ART DIRECTOR/DESIGNER/ILLUSTRATOR: HELENA MODÉER PHOTOGRAPHER: MAX BROUWERS
MODEL: SIMON DESIGN FIRM: WUNDERMAN CATO JOHNSON AB CLIENT: APPLE COMPUTER COUNTRY: SWEDEN

■ (OPPOSITE TOP) Art Director/Designer: LANA RIGSBY Illustrator: ANDY DEARWATER Photographer: ARTHUR MEYERSON Model: SCOTT KOHN Design Firm: RIGSBY DESIGN, INC. Client: PRESENTATION TECHNOLOGIES Country: USA ■ (OPPOSITE BOTTOM) Art Directors/Designers: STAVROS VIDALIS, FRÉDÉRIC GRAF Illustrator: TARKIN Photographer: STAVROS VIDALIS Model: LAURENT VAUCLAIR Design Firm: INDIGO Client: SWATCH SA Country: SWITZERLAND ■ (THIS PAGE) Art Director/Designer: FRANK HAVEMAN Photographer: RANDY HARQUAIL Model: SABINA Design Firm: CORPORATE DESIGN GROUP Client: NORTHERN TELECOM Country: CANADA

ART DIRECTORS/DESIGNERS: JOCHEN DRIEMEL, GERHARD SCHIELEIN
PHOTOGRAPHER: JOCHEN HARDER
MODEL: TATJANA
MAKE-UP ARTIST: WAYNE NYBERG
DESIGN FIRM/CLIENT: IDEEN IN WORT + SCHRIFT
COUNTRY: GERMANY

ART DIRECTORS/DESIGNERS: KRISTIN SOMMESE, LANNY SOMMESE
ILLUSTRATOR: LANNY SOMMESE
PHOTOGRAPHER: KRISTIN SOMMESE
DESIGN FIRM: SOMMESE DESIGN
CLIENT: HAPPY VALLEY BREWERY
COUNTRY: USA

ART DIRECTOR/DESIGNER: LANA RIGSBY
PHOTOGRAPHER: CHRIS SHINN
MODEL: LANA RIGSBY
DESIGN FIRM: RIGSBY DESIGN, INC.
CLIENT: ZOOT RESTAURANT
COUNTRY: USA

■ (ABOVE) ART DIRECTOR: MARY HAUVILLER ILLUSTRATOR: AGNES AUDRAS (REP. CLAIRE PRÉBOIS) PHOTOGRAPHER: ERIC AUDRAS MODEL: STÉFANIE FAUST CLIENT: VILLEROY & BOCH COUNTRY: FRANCE ■ (OPPOSITE TOP) ART DIRECTION/DESIGN: FHA DESIGN PHOTOGRAPHER: GREG DELVES DESIGN FIRM: FHA DESIGN CLIENT: TOP OF THE BAY COUNTRY: AUSTRALIA ■ (OPPOSITE BOTTOM) ART DIRECTOR/DESIGNER/ILLUSTRATOR/MODEL: FERNANDO MEDINA PHOTOGRAPHER: TRIOM DESIGN DESIGN FIRM: TRIOM DESIGN CLIENT: EL CINEMATOGRAFO COUNTRY: SPAIN

ART DIRECTOR/DESIGNER: PAUL KOELEMAN
PHOTOGRAPHER: COR VAN GASTEL
DESIGN FIRM: STUDIO PAUL KOELEMAN
CLIENT: BLOOMINGDALE'S
COUNTRY: USA

ART DIRECTOR/DESIGNER: JEAN-PIERRE DATTNER
PHOTOGRAPHER: JOSÉ CRESPO
MODEL: PIERRE GAFFNER
CLIENT: SGA MANAGEMENT SA
COUNTRY: SWITZERLAND

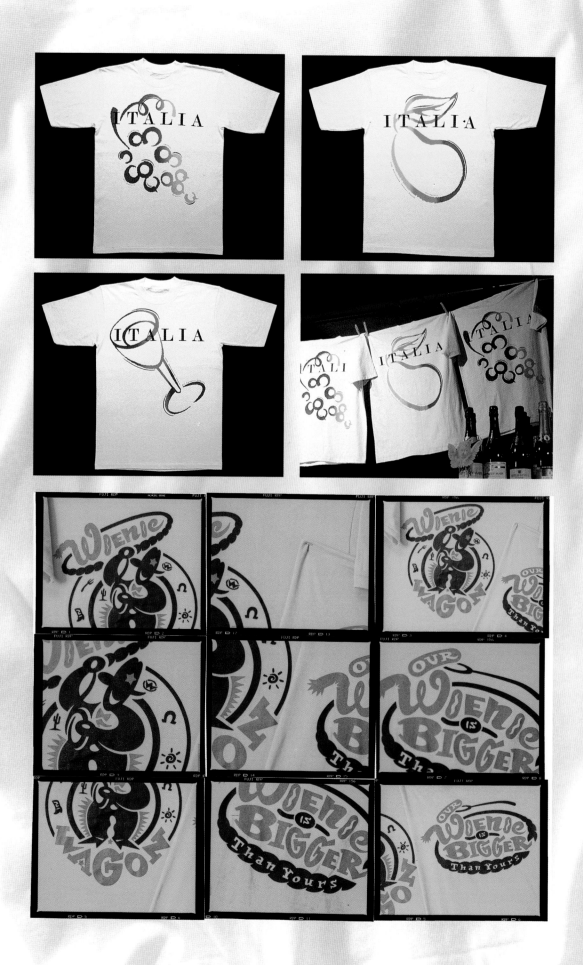

(OPPOSITE PAGE) ■ 1-4 ART DIRECTOR: JACK ANDERSON DESIGNERS: JACK ANDERSON, JULIA LAPINE ILLUSTRATOR: JULIA LAPINE DESIGN FIRM: HORNALL ANDERSON DESIGN WORKS CLIENT: ITALIA COUNTRY: USA ■ 5 ART DIRECTOR: JOHN SAYLES DESIGNER: JOHN SAYLES ILLUSTRATOR: JOHN SAYLES PHOTOGRAPHER: JOHN CLARK DESIGN FIRM: SAYLES GRAPHIC DESIGN CLIENT: WIENIE WAGON COUNTRY: USA ■ (ABOVE) ART DIRECTOR: SHARON OCCHIPINTI DESIGNER: SHARON OCCHIPINTI PHOTOGRAPHER: ROY GUMPEL MODEL: HAROLD HEFEL DESIGN FIRM: DDB NEEDHAM WORLDWIDE MARKETING CLIENT: NATIONAL FEDERATION OF COFFEE GROWERS OF COLOMBIA COUNTRY: USA

ART DIRECTOR/DESIGNER: JOE DUFFY
ILLUSTRATOR: LYNN SCHULTE
DESIGN FIRM: DUFFY DESIGN GROUP
CLIENT: CITY OF MINNEAPOLIS
COUNTRY: USA

ART DIRECTOR: JOE DUFFY
DESIGNER: SHARON WERNER
ILLUSTRATORS: SHARON WERNER, LYNN SCHULTE
DESIGN FIRM: DUFFY DESIGN GROUP
CLIENT: FALLON MCELLIGOTT
COUNTRY: USA

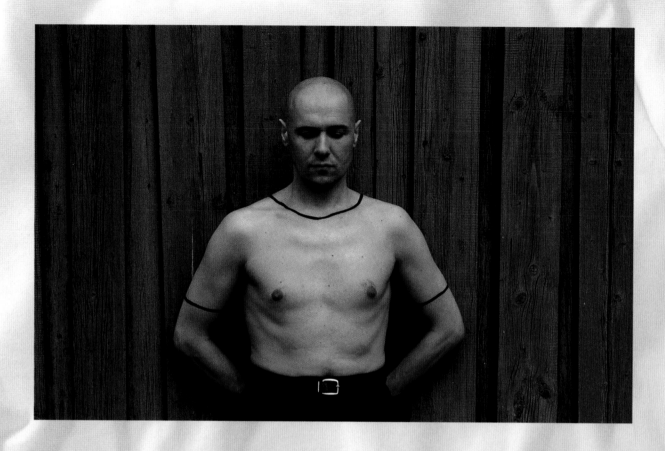

DESIGNER: VLADIMIR CHAIKA
PHOTOGRAPHER: VLADIMIR CHAIKA
MODEL: VLADIMIR CHAIKA
COUNTRY: RUSSIA

DESIGNER: VLADIMIR CHAIKA

PHOTOGRAPHER: VLADIMIR CHAIKA

MODEL: VLADIMIR CHAIKA

COUNTRY: RUSSIA

ART DIRECTOR/DESIGNER: STEPHAN AUER

PHOTOGRAPHER: DANIEL MAYER

MODEL: FLORA

DESIGN FIRM/CLIENT: STEPHAN AUER WERBUNG

COUNTRY: GERMANY

ART DIRECTORS/DESIGNERS: BOB HAMBLY, BARBARA WOOLLEY
ILLUSTRATOR: BOB HAMBLY
PHOTOGRAPHER: SIMON TANENBAUM
DESIGN FIRM/CLIENT: HAMBLY & WOOLLEY INC.
COUNTRY: CANADA

ART DIRECTOR/DESIGNER: JOHN SAYLES
ILLUSTRATOR: JOHN SAYLES
PHOTOGRAPHER: JOHN CLARK
DESIGN FIRM/CLIENT: SAYLES GRAPHIC DESIGN
COUNTRY: USA

DESIGNER: TOM SAPUTO
PHOTOGRAPHER: MICHAEL RUPPERT
DESIGN FIRM/CLIENT: TEAM ONE ADVERTISING
COUNTRY: USA

DESIGNERS

(THIS SPREAD)
ART DIRECTOR/DESIGNER: CLIVE GAY
PHOTOGRAPHER: DAVE GARLICK
MODELS: BELINDA TINKHOF, JOHN MEYER
DESIGN FIRM/CLIENT: TRADEMARK DESIGN LIMITED
COUNTRY: GREAT BRITAIN

ART DIRECTOR/DESIGNER: JACK SUMMERFORD
PHOTOGRAPHER: STEWART COHEN
MODEL: JACK SUMMERFORD
DESIGN FIRM/CLIENT: SUMMERFORD DESIGN INC.
COUNTRY: USA

ART DIRECTOR/DESIGNER: JACK SUMMERFORD
PHOTOGRAPHER: STEWART COHEN
MODEL: JACK SUMMERFORD
DESIGN FIRM/CLIENT: SUMMERFORD DESIGN INC.
COUNTRY: USA

ART DIRECTORS/DESIGNERS: ROBYNNE RAYE, MICHAEL STRASSBURGER
PHOTOGRAPHER: REX RYSTEDT
MODELS: ROBYNNE RAYE, MICHAEL STRASSBURGER
DESIGN FIRM/CLIENT: MODERN DOG
COUNTRY: USA

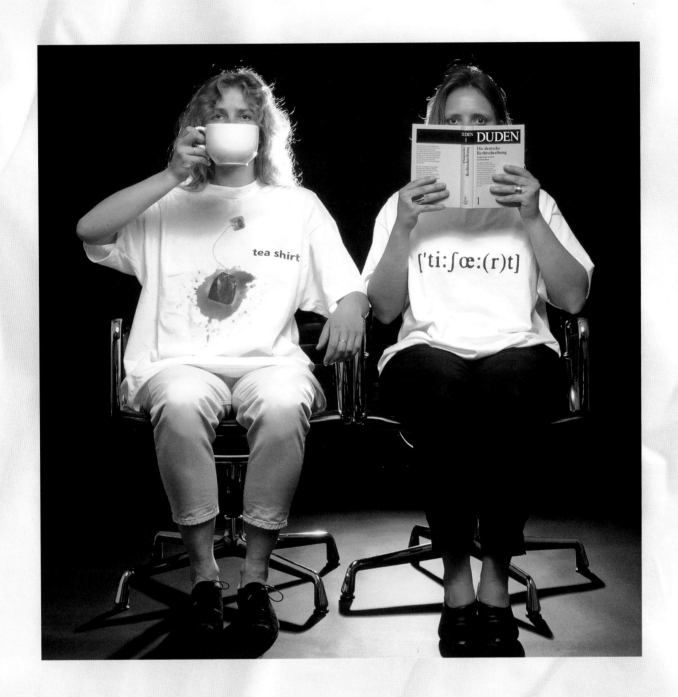

DESIGNER: UDO BECHMANN
PHOTOGRAPHER: UDO BECHMANN
MODELS: IRIS UTIKAL, THEKLA HALBACH
CLIENT: UDO BECHMANN
COUNTRY: GERMANY

ART DIRECTOR: JOSE SERRANO
ILLUSTRATOR: TRACY SABIN
PHOTOGRAPHER: STEVEN TEX
MODEL: MARGARET TEX
DESIGN FIRM: MIRES DESIGN, INC.
COUNTRY: USA

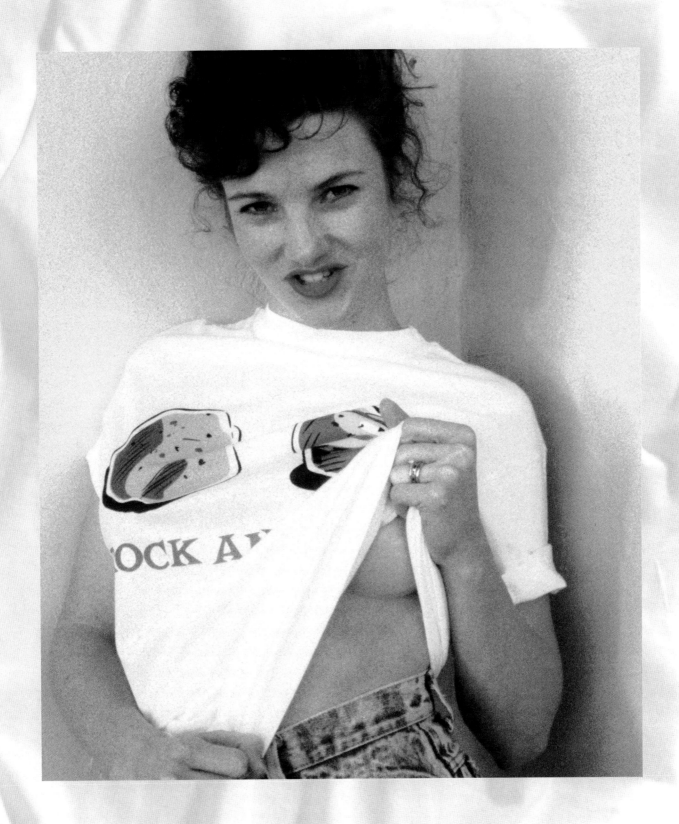

ART DIRECTOR: JOSE SERRANO
ILLUSTRATOR: TRACY SABIN
PHOTOGRAPHER: STEVEN TEX
MODEL: MARGARET TEX
DESIGN FIRM: MIRES DESIGN, INC.
COUNTRY: USA

ART DIRECTOR/DESIGNER: THOMAS FEICHT
PHOTOGRAPHER: KLAUS WEDDIG
MODEL: THOMAS FEICHT
DESIGN FIRM: TRUST
COUNTRY: GERMANY

ART DIRECTOR: UWE LOESCH
DESIGNERS: IRIS UTIKAL, MICHAEL GAIS
PHOTOGRAPHER: UDO BECHMANN
MODEL: MICHAEL GAIS
DESIGN FIRM: LOESCH
COUNTRY: GERMANY

ART DIRECTOR/DESIGNER: ERIKA A. VARMING

PHOTOGRAPHERS: MARIE LÜBECKER, SOREN VARMING

MODELS: ERIKA VARMING, SOREN VARMING

DESIGN FIRM: ERIKA A. VARMING TEXTILE DESIGN

COUNTRY: DENMARK

ART DIRECTOR/DESIGNER: ERIKA A. VARMING
PHOTOGRAPHERS: MARIE LÜBECKER, SOREN VARMING
MODEL: ERIKA VARMING
DESIGN FIRM: ERIKA A. VARMING TEXTILE DESIGN
COUNTRY: DENMARK

ART DIRECTOR/DESIGNER: YVAN HOSTETTLER
ILLUSTRATOR: BUCHE
PHOTOGRAPHER: FABIEN CRUCHON
MODEL: YVAN HOSTETTLER
DESIGN FIRM: GRAPHIC EMOTION
COUNTRY: SWITZERLAND

ART DIRECTOR/DESIGNER: YVAN HOSTETTLER
ILLUSTRATOR: BUCHE
PHOTOGRAPHER: FABIEN CRUCHON
MODEL: YVAN HOSTETTLER
DESIGN FIRM: GRAPHIC EMOTION
COUNTRY: SWITZERLAND

ART DIRECTOR/DESIGNER: YVAN HOSTETTLER
ILLUSTRATOR: BUCHE
PHOTOGRAPHER: FABIEN CRUCHON
MODEL: YVAN HOSTETTLER
DESIGN FIRM: GRAPHIC EMOTION
COUNTRY: SWITZERLAND

ART DIRECTOR/DESIGNER: YVAN HOSTETTLER
ILLUSTRATOR: MUSATI
PHOTOGRAPHER: FABIEN CRUCHON
MODEL: YVAN HOSTETTLER
DESIGN FIRM: GRAPHIC EMOTION
COUNTRY: SWITZERLAND

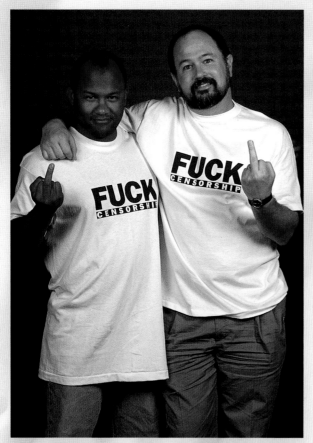

(OPPOSITE PAGE) ■ **1** Art Director/Designer: GUNNAR SWANSON Photographer: ANTHONY NEX Models: GARLAND KIRKPATRICK, GUNNAR SWANSON Design Firm/Client: GUNNAR SWANSON DESIGN OFFICE Country: USA ■ **2** Art Director: RAOUL TOMADA Designers: JAKOB NASER, RAOUL TOMADA Illustrator: MICHAEL UNGER Photographer: JÖRG FICHNA Model: NICOLE BELMANN Design Firm/Client: BASIC DESIGN Country: GERMANY ■ **3** Designer: ALEXANDER STROHMAIER Photographer: STEFAN JETTER Model: SUMITRA NANJUNDAN Country: AUSTRIA ■ **4** Art Director/Designer/Illustrator: ALEXANDER GELMAN Photographer: MYRIAM MORGENSTERN Model: ALEXANDER GELMAN Country: ISRAEL ■ (THIS PAGE) Art Director: WOODY PIRTLE Designer: WOODY PIRTLE Design Firm: PENTAGRAM DESIGN Client: PENTAGRAM DESIGN Countries: USA AND GREAT BRITAIN

■ (ABOVE) DESIGNER/ILLUSTRATOR/PHOTOGRAPHER: ANDREY LOGVIN MODEL: MASHA LOGVIN DESIGN FIRM: LOGVIN DESIGN COUNTRY: RUSSIA ■ (OPPOSITE PAGE) ART DIRECTOR/DESIGNER/ILLUSTRATOR: ALEXANDER GELMAN PHOTOGRAPHER: MYRIAM MORGENSTERN MODEL: ALEXANDER GELMAN COUNTRY: ISRAEL ■ (FOLLOWING SPREAD LEFT) ART DIRECTOR: BERND KELLER PHOTOGRAPHER: GOTTHART A. EICHHORN DESIGN FIRM/ CLIENT: KELLER ASSOZIIERTE COUNTRY: GERMANY ■ (FOLLOWING SPREAD RIGHT) ART DIRECTOR/DESIGNER/ ILLUSTRATOR: WENDY TANCOCK PHOTOGRAPHER: SIMON TANENBAUM DESIGN FIRM/CLIENT: WENDY TANCOCK DESIGN + ILLUSTRATION COUNTRY: CANADA

■ (OPPOSITE PAGE) ART DIRECTOR: PETER KRINNINGER DESIGNER: MAX LOCHNER PHOTOGRAPHER: PETER KRINNINGER MODELS: THERESA, VERENA CLIENT: MAX MAD HOUSE COUNTRY: GERMANY ■ (ABOVE) ART DIRECTORS/ DESIGNERS/MODELS: BOB HAMBLY, BARBARA WOOLLEY ILLUSTRATOR: BOB HAMBLY PHOTOGRAPHER: SIMON TANENBAUM DESIGN FIRM: HAMBLY & WOOLLEY COUNTRY: CANADA ■ (FOLLOWING SPREAD) 1 DESIGNER/MODEL: MONICA MACHADO PHOTOGRAPHER: MARCELO MAGALHAES DESIGN FIRM: PREMIAIA DESIGN COUNTRY: BRASIL ■ 2 ART DIRECTOR: RAOUL TOMADA DESIGNERS: JAKOB NASER, RAOUL TOMADA ILLUSTRATOR: MICHAEL UNGER PHOTOGRAPHER: JÖRG FICHNA MODEL: NICOLE BELMANN DESIGN FIRM/CLIENT: BASIC DESIGN COUNTRY: GERMANY ■ 3 ART DIRECTOR/DESIGNER/ILLUSTRATOR: BARRIE TUCKER PHOTOGRAPHER: STEVE KEOUGH MODEL: EUGENE LOH DESIGN FIRM: TUCKER DESIGN CLIENT: ALLIANCE GRAPHIQUE INTERNATIONALE COUNTRY: SWITZERLAND ■ 4 ART DIRECTOR/ DESIGNER/PHOTOGRAPHER/MODEL: FREDERIC LECHEVALLIER COUNTRY: FRANCE ■ 5 ART DIRECTION/DESIGN/ILLUSTRATION: T-SHIRT-KLUB PHOTOGRAPHER: KNUT GROEGER MODELS: MEMBERS OF THE "T-SHIRT-KLUB" COUNTRY: GERMANY

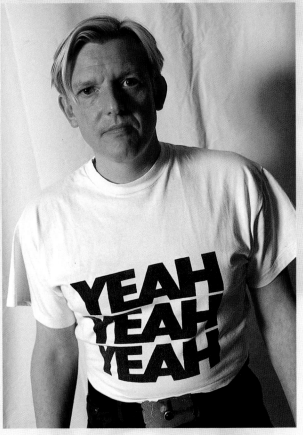

ART DIRECTOR: LO BREIER

DESIGNER: ECKE BONK

PHOTOGRAPHER: JULIA HOERSCH

MODELS: MITSCHI KÖHLER, CHRISTIAN POTT, RALF DICK, IRINA HINZ

DESIGN FIRM/CLIENT: BÜRO X

COUNTRY: GERMANY

ART DIRECTOR/DESIGNER: ALAN J. KEGLER
PHOTOGRAPHER: R.C. KRATT
MODEL: DOUG LEVERE
DESIGN FIRM: COURAGE DESIGN
COUNTRY: USA

DESIGNERS: MARIO JAHNS, KALLE WALLAU
PHOTOGRAPHER: KLAUS QUAUKE
MODELS: KALLE WALLAU, MARIO JAHNS
CLIENT: STADT DÜSSELDORF
COUNTRY: GERMANY

ART DIRECTOR/DESIGNER: SANTIAGO POL
ILLUSTRATOR: JUAN JOSE ABREU
PHOTOGRAPHER: JUAN CARLOS MORATINOS
DESIGN FIRM: POLSTER PUBLICITY
CLIENT: FUNDATENEO FESTIVAL
COUNTRY: VENEZUELA

ART DIRECTOR/DESIGNER/ILLUSTRATOR: JOHN SAYLES
PHOTOGRAPHER: JOHN CLARK
MODEL: MELINDA SORENSON
DESIGN FIRM: SAYLES GRAPHIC DESIGN
CLIENT: SUN MICROSYSTEMS
COUNTRY: USA

ART DIRECTOR/DESIGNER/ILLUSTRATO: FERNANDO MEDINA
PHOTOGRAPH: TRIOM DESIGN
MODEL: FERNANDO MEDINA
DESIGN FIRM: TRIOM DESIGN
CLIENT: CANADIAN NATIONAL EXPO 86
COUNTRY: CANADA

ART DIRECTOR: JACK ANDERSON
DESIGNERS: JACK ANDERSON, JANI DREWFS, DAVID BATES
ILLUSTRATORS: JACK ANDERSON, DAVID BATES
DESIGN FIRM: HORNALL ANDERSON DESIGN WORKS
CLIENT: CASCADE BICYCLE CLUB
COUNTRY: USA

ART DIRECTOR: JACK ANDERSON
DESIGNERS: JACK ANDERSON, BRIAN O'NEILL
DESIGN FIRM: HORNALL ANDERSON DESIGN WORKS
CLIENT: GANG OF SEVEN
COUNTRY: USA

(THIS SPREAD)
ART DIRECTOR: MARK SACKETT
DESIGNERS: MARK SACKETT, WAYNE SAKAMOTO
ILLUSTRATORS: MARK SACKETT, WAYNE SAKAMOTO, CHRIS VARYAN
DESIGN FIRM: SACKETT DESIGN
COUNTRY: USA

ART DIRECTORS: DOUG THOMPKIN, WAYNE KOGAN
DESIGNER/ILLUSTRATOR: MICHAEL SCHWAB
PHOTOGRAPHER: TOSCANI/ROBERTO CARRA
CLIENT: ESPRIT
COUNTRY: USA

(OPPOSITE PAGE)
ART DIRECTOR/DESIGNER: SUSAN SCOTT
PHOTOGRAPHER: JAMES ST. LAURENT
MAKE-UP ARTIST: YVES LE BLANC
MODEL: MIRI JEDEIKIN
CLIENT: STEFANEL CANADA
COUNTRY: CANADA

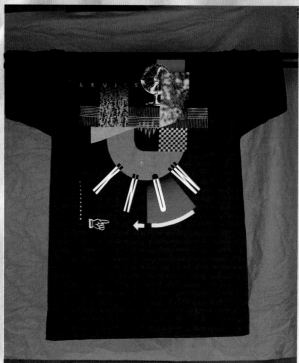

ART DIRECTORS: SANDRA HORVAT VALLELY (1, 4), TROY ALDERS (2), COLIN BIRDSEYE (3)
DESIGNERS/ILLUSTRATORS: TIM MITOMA (1, 4), BILL BRENT (2), CARIN REHBINDER (3)
DESIGN FIRM: WINTERLAND PRODUCTIONS
CLIENTS: LEVI STRAUSS & CO. (1, 3, 4), DREAD ZEPPELIN (2)
COUNTRY: USA

ART DIRECTOR: SANDRA HORVAT VALLELY
DESIGNER/ILLUSTRATOR: RAYMOND LARRETT
DESIGN FIRM: WINTERLAND PRODUCTIONS
CLIENTS: LEVI STRAUSS & CO.
COUNTRY: USA

ART DIRECTOR: PETER G. UZIEBLO
DESIGNER: CONTROLLED BURN ACTIVEWEAR
PHOTOGRAPHER: PETER G. UZIEBLO
COUNTRY: CANADA

ART DIRECTOR: JOSE SERRANO
ILLUSTRATOR: TRACY SABIN
PHOTOGRAPHER: STEVEN TEX
MODEL: MARGARET TEX
DESIGN FIRM: MIRES DESIGN INC.
CLIENT: TEE SHIRT CO.
COUNTRY: USA

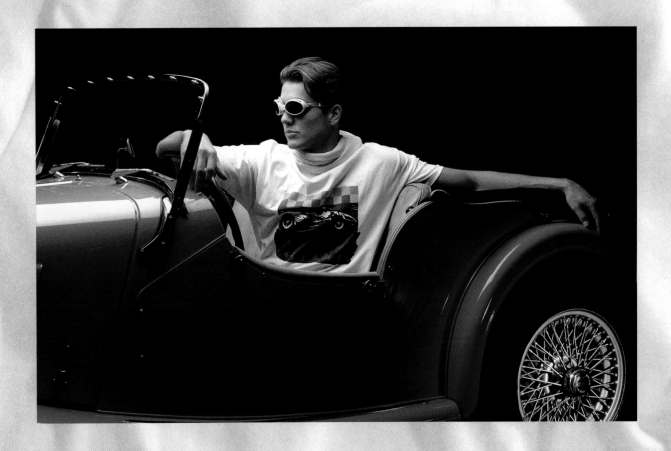

■ (OPPOSITE PAGE, TOP) ART DIRECTOR/DESIGNER/PHOTOGRAPHER: B. MARTIN PEDERSEN ILLUSTRATOR: RON DAROS MODELS: CHRISTOPHER, SEBASTIAN, JANE, SUSAN CLIENT: EAST ENDER DESIGN COUNTRY: USA ■ (OPPOSITE PAGE, BOTTOM) ART DIRECTOR: MARK DELLPLAIN DESIGNERS/ILLUSTRATORS: ROBYNNE RAYE, VITTORIO COSTARELLA PHOTOGRAPHER: LISA MULHOLLAND DESIGN FIRM: MODERN DOG CLIENT: M'OTTO RED DOT COUNTRY: USA ■ (ABOVE) DESIGNER: SUSAN SCOTT PHOTOGRAPHER: JAMES ST. LAURENT MODEL: RYAN MICHAELS CLIENT: STEFANEL CANADA COUNTRY: CANADA

■ (THIS PAGE, TOP, BOTH IMAGES) ART DIRECTORS: LINDA KONDO, STEPHANIE WADE DESIGNERS: LINDA KONDO, STEPHANIE WADE PHOTOGRAPHER: PETER RICE DESIGN FIRM: CLIFFORD SELBERT DESIGN, INC. CLIENT: CONVERSE INC. COUNTRY: USA ■ (THIS PAGE, BOTTOM) ART DIRECTOR: JACK ANDERSON DESIGNERS: JACK

ANDERSON, DENISE WEIR, JULIA LAPINE, BRIAN O'NEILL Design Firm: HORNALL ANDERSON DESIGN WORKS
Client: K2 CORPORATION Country: USA ■ (ABOVE) Art Director: MARK DELLPLAIN Designer: VITTORIO COSTA-
RELLA Photographer: LISA MULHOLLAND Design Firm: MODERN DOG Client: M'OTTO RED DOT Country: USA

ART DIRECTOR/DESIGNER: MATTHIAS BRUCKLACHER
PHOTOGRAPH: ANDREAS JUNG
MODEL: MARY BUCK
CLIENT: SCOOZI
COUNTRY: GERMANY

■ (ABOVE, LEFT) ART DIRECTOR: JOHN SAYLES DESIGNER: JOHN SAYLES ILLUSTRATOR: JOHN SAYLES PHOTOGRAPHER: JOHN CLARK DESIGN FIRM: SAYLES GRAPHIC DESIGN CLIENT: SCHAFFER'S TUXEDO EXPRESS COUNTRY: USA ■ (ABOVE RIGHT) ART DIRECTOR/DESIGNER: MICHAEL CRONAN PHOTOGRAPHER: JOCK MCDONALD MODEL: BRITTA COX DESIGN FIRM: CRONAN DESIGN CLIENT: CRONAN ARTEFACT COUNTRY: USA ■ (OPPOSITE PAGE) ART DIRECTOR: BETT LALOUM PHOTOGRAPHER: ERIC AUDRAS DESIGN FIRM: GREY CLIENT: GEPY COUNTRY: FRANCE

ART DIRECTOR: ELA BAUER

DESIGNER: ROLAND SCHNEIDER

PHOTOGRAPHER: ROLAND SCHNEIDER

DESIGN FIRM: BAUERS BÜRO

CLIENT: FHS ROSENHEIM: SZENOGRAFIE

COUNTRY: GERMANY

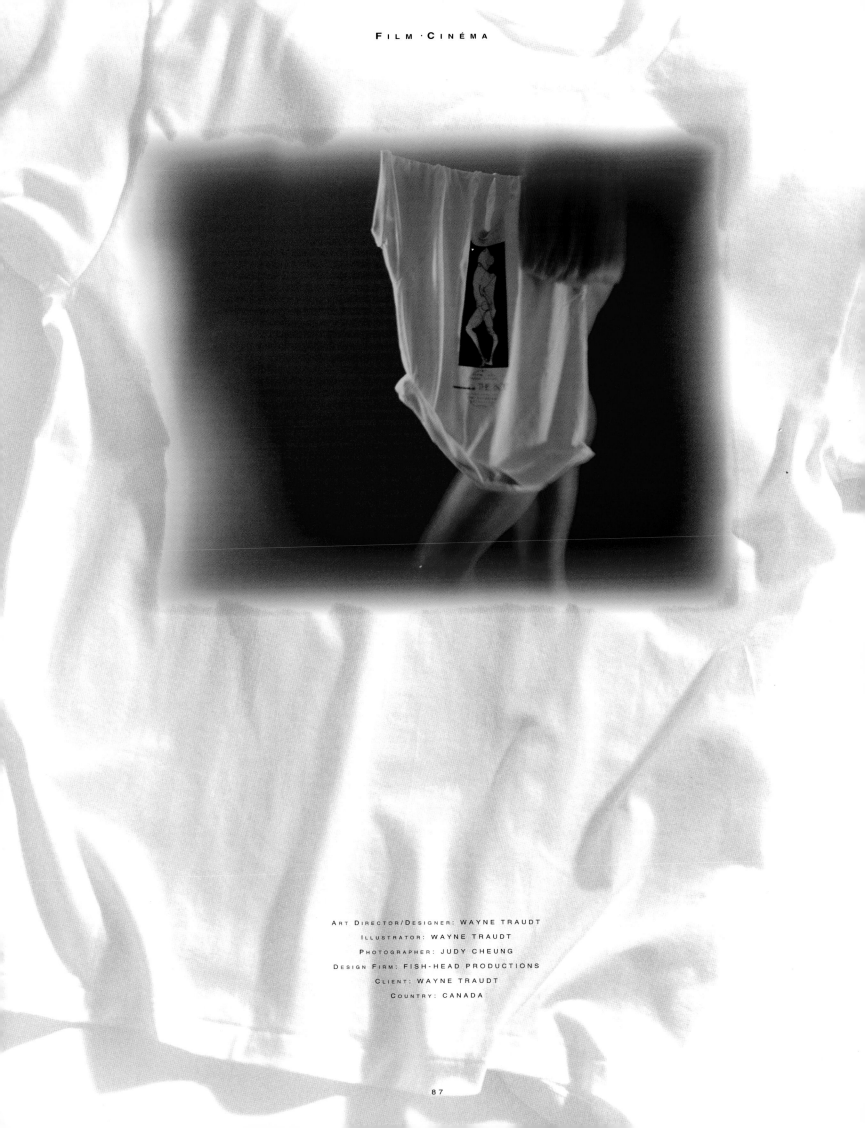

ART DIRECTOR/DESIGNER: WAYNE TRAUDT
ILLUSTRATOR: WAYNE TRAUDT
PHOTOGRAPHER: JUDY CHEUNG
DESIGN FIRM: FISH-HEAD PRODUCTIONS
CLIENT: WAYNE TRAUDT
COUNTRY: CANADA

ART DIRECTOR: CHARLES S. ANDERSON
DESIGNERS: DANIEL OLSON, CHARLES S. ANDERSON
DESIGN FIRM: C.S. ANDERSON DESIGN
CLIENT: HOLLYWOOD PARAMOUNT PRODUCTS
COUNTRY: USA

ART DIRECTOR/DESIGNER: LOUIS OCEPEK
PHOTOGRAPHER: MICHAEL LAURANCE
MODEL: ANTONYA NELSON
CLIENT: MESILLA VALLEY FILM SOCIETY
COUNTRY: USA

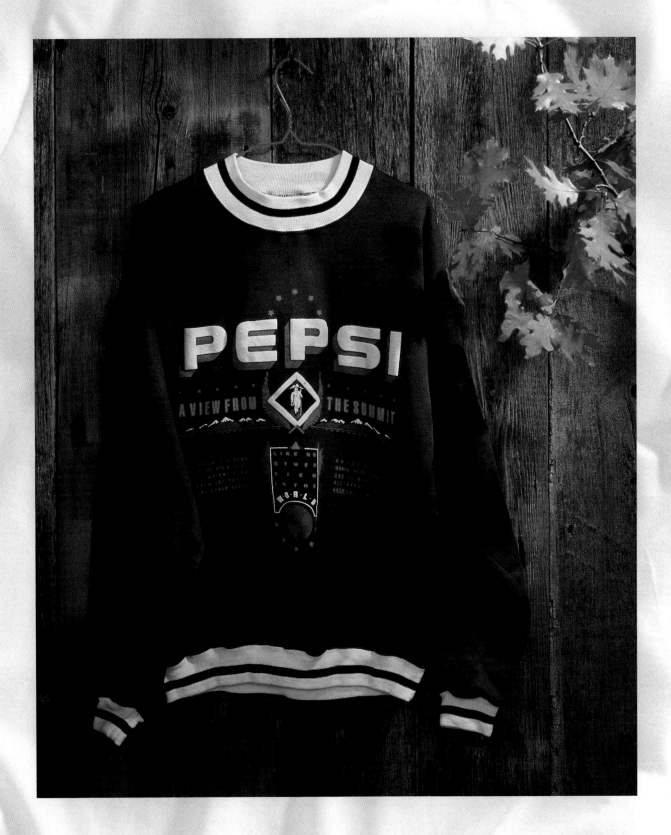

ART DIRECTOR/DESIGNER: MARK SACKETT
ILLUSTRATOR: MARK SACKETT
DESIGN FIRM: SACKETT DESIGN
CLIENT: PEPSI
COUNTRY: USA

■ (THIS PAGE) ART DIRECTOR: NEIL SHAKERY DESIGNER: NEIL SHAKERY PHOTOGRAPHER: BOB ESPARZA MODEL: LESLIE MCDOUGALL DESIGN FIRM: PENTAGRAM DESIGN CLIENT: RONNYBROOK FARM DAIRY COUNTRY: USA ■ (OPPOSITE PAGE) ART DIRECTOR/DESIGNER: DRAGUTIN DADO KOVACEVIC ILLUSTRATOR: DRAGUTIN DADO KOVACEVIC PHOTOGRAPHER: FJODOR FATICIC DESIGN FIRM: DESIGN ART CLIENT: ZDJELAREVIC COUNTRY: CROATIA

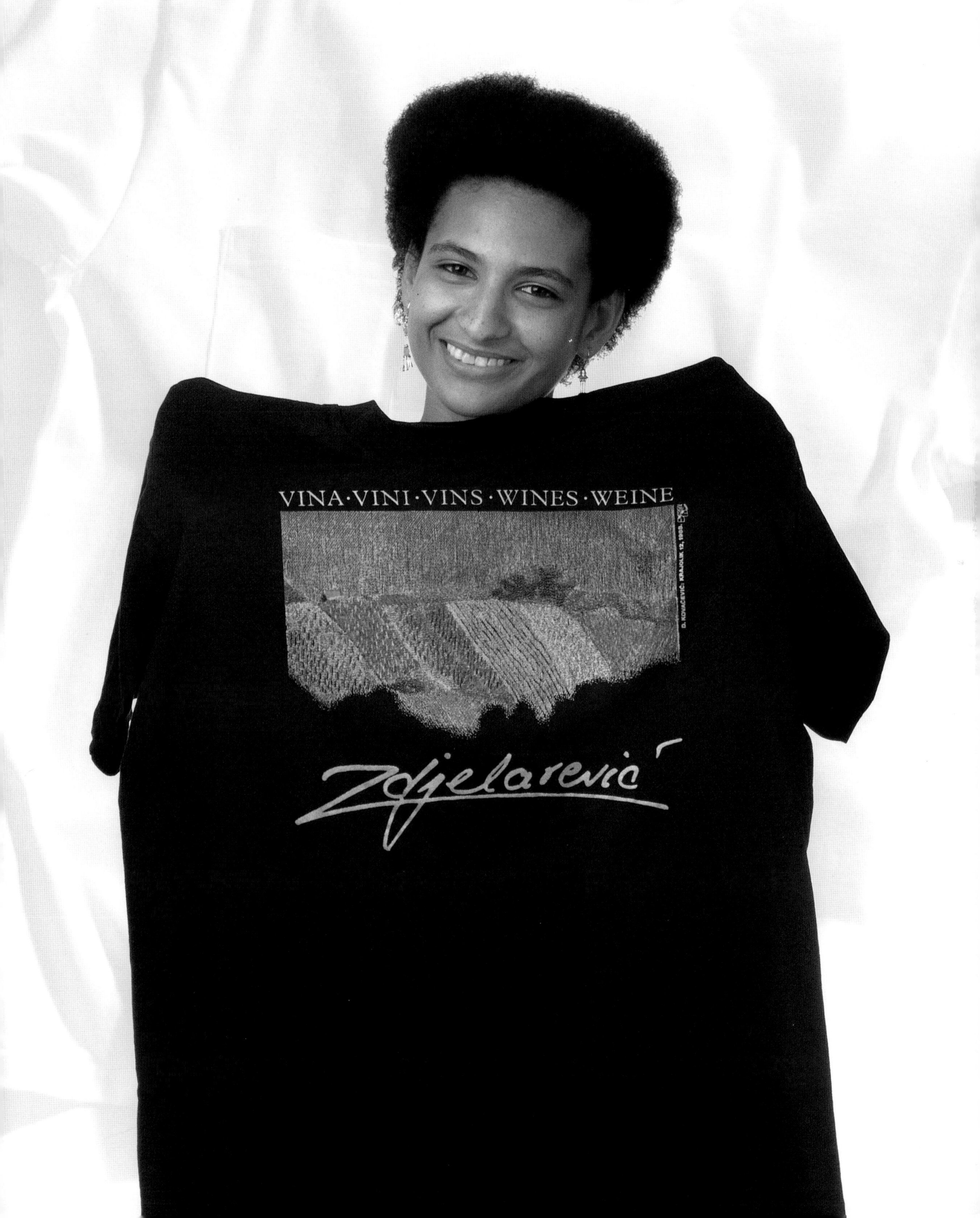
VINA·VINI·VINS·WINES·WEINE
Zdjelarević

ILLUSTRATOR: MARTIN HUTZLER
PHOTOGRAPHER: HELMUT BAUER
MODEL: GERHARD KUNZ
COUNTRY: GERMANY

DESIGNER: CHRISTOPH ZEHM
PHOTOGRAPHER: JENS LIEBRECHT
MODEL: CLAUDIUS SCHIFFER
CLIENT: PALAST PROMOTION GMBH
COUNTRY: GERMANY

DESIGNER: LYNN PUTNEY
PHOTOGRAPHER: GENE YOUNG
CLIENT: NATIONAL MUSEUM OF AMERICAN ART, SMITHSONIAN INSTITUTION
COUNTRY: USA

DESIGNER: LYNN PUTNEY
PHOTOGRAPHER: GENE YOUNG
CLIENT: NATIONAL MUSEUM OF AMERICAN ART, SMITHSONIAN INSTITUTION
COUNTRY: USA

ART DIRECTOR: JEAN MORIN
DESIGNER: ALAIN ROCHON
PHOTOGRAPHER: CHRISTINE GUEST/THE MONTREAL MUSEUM OF FINE ARTS
DESIGN FIRM: AXION, INC.
CLIENT: THE MONTREAL MUSEUM OF FINE ARTS
COUNTRY: CANADA

ART DIRECTOR: KIT HINRICHS
DESIGNER: SUSAN TSUCHIYA
PHOTOGRAPHER: BARRY ROBINSON
MODEL: SHELLY REILLY
DESIGN FIRM: PENTAGRAM DESIGN
CLIENT: MUSEUM OF CONTEMPORARY ART, SAN DIEGO
COUNTRY: USA

ART DIRECTOR/DESIGNER: KIT HINRICHS
PHOTOGRAPHER: BOB ESPARZA
MODEL: LESLIE MCDOUGALL
DESIGN FIRM: PENTAGRAM DESIGN
CLIENT: CALIFORNIA CRAFTS MUSEUM
COUNTRY: USA

ART DIRECTOR: KIT HINRICHS
DESIGNER: MARK SELFE
PHOTOGRAPHER: BOB ESPARZA
MODEL: LESLIE MCDOUGALL
DESIGN FIRM: PENTAGRAM DESIGN
CLIENT: PACIFIC DESIGN CENTER
COUNTRY: USA

ART DIRECTOR: JEAN-JACQUES TACHDJIAN
PHOTOGRAPHER: JEAN-PIERRE DUPLAN
MODEL: EL ROTRINGO
DESIGN FIRM: I COMME IMAGE
CLIENT: KINGSIZE
COUNTRY: FRANCE

ART DIRECTOR: JEAN-JACQUES TACHDJIAN
PHOTOGRAPHER: JEAN-PIERRE DUPLAN
MODEL: NANOU
DESIGN FIRM: I COMME IMAGE
CLIENT: DANCETERIA RECORDS
COUNTRY: FRANCE

(THIS SPREAD)
ART DIRECTOR/DESIGNER: NIKLAUS TROXLER
PHOTOGRAPHER: EMANUEL AMMON
MODELS: PAULA, ANNIK, NIKLAUS TROXLER, EMS TROXLER
CLIENTS: JAZZ IN WILLISAU, UMWELT UND BESINNUNGSTAGE LUZERN, KUNZ-SPORT
COUNTRY: SWITZERLAND

ART DIRECTOR/DESIGNER/ILLUSTRATOR: GYÖRGY KEMÉNY
PHOTOGRAPHER: GYÖRGY KEMÉNY
CLIENT: GYÖRGY KEMÉNY
COUNTRY: HUNGARY

ART DIRECTOR: MARGUS HAAVAMÄGI
DESIGNER/ILLUSTRATOR: MARGUS HAAVAMÄGI
PHOTOGRAPHER: MARGUS HAAVAMÄGI
CLIENT: SAXAPPEAL BAND VILLU VESKI
COUNTRY: ESTONIA

DESIGNER: ROBERT L. PETERS
PHOTOGRAPHER: PAUL MARTENS
MODEL: "A.J."
DESIGN FIRM: CIRCLE DESIGN
CLIENT: THE LAB WORKS
COUNTRY: CANADA

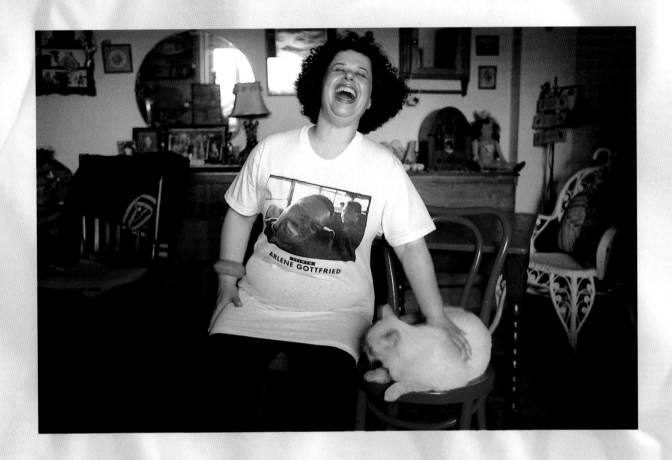

DESIGNER: LOIS CARLO
PHOTOGRAPHER/MODEL: ARLENE GOTTFRIED
CLIENT: ARLENE GOTTFRIED
COUNTRY: USA

ART DIRECTORS: SASHA HAETTENSCHWEILER, THOMAS RHYNER, JAN KROHN

PHOTOGRAPHER: DANIEL VALANCE

CLIENT: HANSJÖRG DETTLING

COUNTRY: SWITZERLAND

ART DIRECTOR/DESIGNER: TODD WATERBURY
ILLUSTRATOR: LYNN SCHULTE
DESIGN FIRM: DUFFY DESIGN GROUP
CLIENT: FOX RIVER PAPER COMPANY
COUNTRY: USA

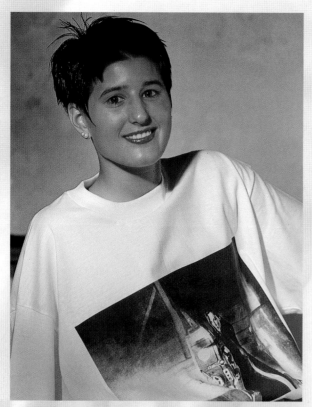

PHOTOGRAPHER: RALF GANTER
MODEL: SILKE S.
COUNTRY: GERMANY

PHOTOGRAPHER: GÜNTER MEMMESHEIMER
MODEL: MICHAEL JARBOE/NO TOYS
COUNTRY: GERMANY

ART DIRECTOR/ILLUSTRATOR: CINDY VAN LING
PHOTOGRAPHER: CINDY VAN LING
MODEL: LIONG LIE
DESIGN FIRM: STUDIO 123 DV
COUNTRY: NETHERLANDS

PHOTOGRAPHER: JOCHEN WALKENHORST
MODEL: MARGRIT HÖGLINGER
COUNTRY: GERMANY

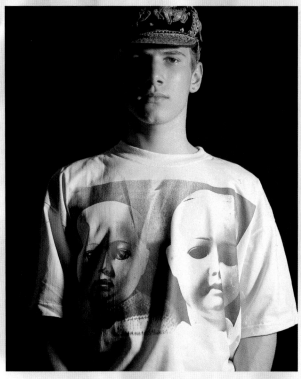

■ (OPPOSITE PAGE) **1** DESIGNER: LENNART FORUP PHOTOGRAPHER: EBBE FORUP MODEL: EBBE FORUP COUNTRY: DENMARK ■ **2** DESIGNER: RAVEN METZNER PHOTOGRAPHER: B. MARTIN PEDERSEN MODEL: CHRISTOPHER CLIENT: SHEILA METZNER COUNTRY: USA ■ **3** DESIGNER: BETTINA BÖHMER PHOTOGRAPHER: BETTINA BÖHMER MODEL: LUKAS WAGNER COUNTRY: GERMANY ■ **4** ART DIRECTOR/ILLUSTRATOR: WERNER GRIEDER PHOTOGRAPHER: HUGO SIEGFRIED MODEL: MARCEL VOGT CLIENT: HUGO SIEGFRIED AG COUNTRY: SWITZERLAND ■ (THIS PAGE) ART DIRECTOR/DESIGNER: BARRIE TUCKER PHOTOGRAPHER: STEVE KEOUGH MODELS: INGA LIDUMS, SUSAN JOY DESIGN FIRM: TUCKER DESIGN PTY LTD. CLIENT: STEVE KEOUGH PHOTOGRAPHY PTY LTD. COUNTRY: AUSTRALIA

ART DIRECTOR: STEVE BROWER
DESIGNER: KAREN COUGHLIN
ILLUSTRATOR: JAMES VICTORE
PHOTOGRAPHER: RANDALL SAUCHUCK
CLIENT: CAROL PUBLISHING GROUP
COUNTRY: USA

ART DIRECTOR/DESIGNER: SYBILLE BOK
PHOTOGRAPHER: KATHARINA EGLAU
MODEL: MICHAEL SONTHEIMER
CLIENT: TAZ, DIE TAGESZEITUNG
COUNTRY: GERMANY

DESIGNER: JOE MILLER
PHOTOGRAPHER: GLENN MATSUMURA
DESIGN FIRM: JOE MILLER'S COMPANY
CLIENT: KSJS PUBLIC RADIO
COUNTRY: USA

DESIGNER: JOE MILLER
PHOTOGRAPHER: GLENN MATSUMURA
DESIGN FIRM: JOE MILLER'S COMPANY
CLIENT: KSJS PUBLIC RADIO
COUNTRY: USA

ART DIRECTOR: PAMELA STRADWICK
DESIGNER: JAMIE AU
PHOTOGRAPHER: PAUL ORENSTEIN
MODEL: ANTHONY
CLIENT: AZTEX
COUNTRY: CANADA

ART DIRECTOR: PAMELA STRADWICK
DESIGNER: JAMIE AU
PHOTOGRAPHER: PAUL ORENSTEIN
MODEL: ANTHONY
CLIENT: AZTEX
COUNTRY: CANADA

ART DIRECTOR/DESIGNER: JOHN SAYLES
ILLUSTRATOR: JOHN SAYLES
PHOTOGRAPHER: JOHN CLARK
DESIGN FIRM/CLIENT: SAYLES GRAPHIC DESIGN
COUNTRY: USA

CREATIVE DIRECTOR/DESIGNER: KENNETH R. COOKE
ILLUSTRATOR: KATHY KOELZER
PHOTOGRAPHER: KENNETH R. COOKE
MODEL: MITCH ZOLLMAN
DESIGN FIRM: SIEGEL & GALE INC.
CLIENT: SOHO TRAINING CENTER
COUNTRY: USA

■ (OPPOSITE PAGE) ART DIRECTOR: MIKE SALISBURY DESIGNER: MIKE SALISBURY ILLUSTRATOR: JACK DENNY
PHOTOGRAPHER: MIKE SALISBURY MODEL: SONNY GARCIA DESIGN FIRM: MIKE SALISBURY COMMUNICATIONS INC.
CLIENT: MCD SPORTSWEAR COUNTRY: USA ■ (THIS PAGE) ART DIRECTORS/DESIGNERS: STAVROS VIDALIS,
FRÉDÉRIC GRAF ILLUSTRATORS: STAVROS VIDALIS, FRÉDÉRIC GRAF, JACKY GUILARTE, D. MAURICE
PHOTOGRAPHER: FRÉDÉRIC GRAF DESIGN FIRM: INDIGO CLIENT: BREITLING SA COUNTRY: SWITZERLAND

■ (ABOVE LEFT) ART DIRECTOR: MIKE SALISBURY PHOTOGRAPHER: MIKE SALISBURY DESIGNER/ILLUSTRATOR: JAY VIGON DESIGN FIRM: MIKE SALISBURY COMMUNICATIONS CLIENT: GOTCHA COUNTRY: USA ■ (ABOVE RIGHT AND OPPOSITE) ART DIRECTOR: ULRICH SCHENKER DESIGNER: RAPHAEL SCHENKER MODEL: RAPHAEL SCHENKER PHOTOGRAPHER: STEPHAN HANSLIN CLIENT: INTERKANTONALE LANDESLOTTERIE COUNTRY: SWITZERLAND

■ (OPPOSITE TOP) CREATIVE DIRECTOR: JOE DUFFY ART DIRECTORS/DESIGNERS: HALEY JOHNSON, JOE DUFFY
ILLUSTRATOR: LYNN SCHULTE DESIGN FIRM: THE DUFFY DESIGN GROUP CLIENT: RUPERT'S NIGHTCLUB COUNTRY:
USA ■ (OPPOSITE BOTTOM) ART DIRECTOR: OSAMU FURUMURA DESIGNER: KENICHI YOSHIDA DESIGN FIRM: SEE-
SAW CLIENT: EVERY BODY CENTER COUNTRY: JAPAN ■ (ABOVE) ART DIRECTOR: RON DUMAS DESIGNER: ROSS
PATRICK ILLUSTRATORS: MIKE FRAISER, DAN MANDISH DESIGN FIRM: NIKE DESIGN CLIENT: NIKE COUNTRY: USA

ART DIRECTOR: SCOTT MIRES
ILLUSTRATOR: TRACY SABIN
DESIGN FIRM: MIRES DESIGN, INC.
CLIENT: FULL BORE SURF SHOP
COUNTRY: USA

ART DIRECTOR: SCOTT MIRES
ILLUSTRATOR: TRACY SABIN
DESIGN FIRM: MIRES DESIGN, INC.
CLIENT: FULL BORE SURF SHOP
COUNTRY: USA

ART DIRECTOR: SCOTT MIRES
ILLUSTRATORS: GERALD BUSTAMANTE
DESIGN FIRM: MIRES DESIGN, INC.
CLIENT: FULL BORE SURF SHOP
COUNTRY: USA

ART DIRECTOR/DESIGNER: JEFF MUNSON
PHOTOGRAPHER: BOB SCHULDT
MODEL: PATRICIA SIMONNET
DESIGN FIRM/CLIENT: SWADDLING CLOTHES
COUNTRY: USA

ILLUSTRATOR/PHOTOGRAPHER: HARALD GOLDHAHN
MODEL: MICHAELA-SUSANNE SAUERWEIN
CLIENT: FIRMA FLACHSEL
COUNTRY: GERMANY

ILLUSTRATOR/PHOTOGRAPHER: HARALD GOLDHAHN
MODEL: MICHAELA-SUSANNE SAUERWEIN
CLIENTS: FIRMA FLACHSEL (TOP), HARALD GOLDHAHN (BOTTOM)
COUNTRY: GERMANY

■ (PAGE 138) ART DIRECTOR: JOSE SERRANO ILLUSTRATOR: GERALD BUSTAMANTE PHOTOGRAPHER: CARL
VANDERSCHUIT MODEL: CURT CAMPBELL DESIGN FIRM: MIRES DESIGN, INC. CLIENT: DELEO CLAY TILE CO.
COUNTRY: USA ■ (PAGE 139) ART DIRECTOR: MICHAELA NEISER DESIGNER: MICHAELA NEISER PHOTOGRAPHER: EMIL
ZANDER MODEL: TERRY O'NEILL CLIENT: HEINRICH SPOERL FABRIK COUNTRY: GERMANY ■ (THIS PAGE) ART

DIRECTOR: CLIFFORD HARVEY DESIGNER: CLIFFORD HARVEY ILLUSTRATOR: EVE FAULKES PHOTOGRAPHER:
CLIFFORD HARVEY MODEL: CLIFFORD HARVEY DESIGN FIRM/CLIENT: OUR DANES MUCHA PRINTS COUNTRY: USA ■
(ABOVE) ART DIRECTOR: JOHN EVANS, LAURIE EVANS DESIGNER: JOHN EVANS ILLUSTRATOR: JOHN EVANS PHOTOG-
RAPHER: LAURIE EVANS MODELS: ERIC, KRISTIN, RACHEL DESIGN FIRM: JOHN EVANS DESIGN COUNTRY: USA

ART DIRECTOR/DESIGNER: KIT HINRICHS
PHOTOGRAPHER: BARRY ROBINSON
MODEL: SUSIE LEVERSEE
DESIGN FIRM: PENTAGRAM DESIGN
CLIENT: ART CENTER
COUNTRY: USA

ART DIRECTOR/DESIGNER: PATRICK SHORT
ILLUSTRATOR: PATRICK SHORT
PHOTOGRAPHER: TODD MCLEOD
MODEL: FAITH MURPHY
DESIGN FIRM: BLACKBIRD DESIGN
CLIENT: NORTH CAROLINA STATE UNIVERSITY
COUNTRY: USA

ART DIRECTOR/DESIGNER/ILLUSTRATOR: JOHN SAYLES
PHOTOGRAPHER: JOHN CLARK
MODEL: MELINDA SORENSON
DESIGN FIRM: SAYLES GRAPHIC DESIGN
CLIENT: VILLANOVA UNIVERSITY
COUNTRY: USA

ART DIRECTOR/DESIGNER/ILLUSTRATOR: JOHN SAYLES
PHOTOGRAPHER: JOHN CLARK
MODEL: GRETCHEN JONES
DESIGN FIRM: SAYLES GRAPHIC DESIGN
CLIENT: DRAKE UNIVERSITY
COUNTRY: USA

ART DIRECTOR: PETER WOOD
DESIGNERS: JAMIE HOBSON, PETER WOOD
ILLUSTRATOR: JAMIE HOBSON
PHOTOGRAPHER: STUART REDLER
DESIGN FIRM: HOBSON/WOOD
CLIENT: COMMON GROUND
COUNTRY: GREAT BRITAIN

PULL OVER

ART DIRECTORS: IRIS UTIKAL, MICHAEL GAIS
PHOTOGRAPHER: UDO BECHMANN
MODEL: IRIS UTIKAL
DESIGN FIRM/CLIENT: U.A.W.G. DESIGN
COUNTRY: GERMANY

CREATIVE DIRECTOR/DESIGNER/ILLUSTRATOR: RUSSELL PIERCE
PHOTOGRAPHER: MARTIN BROWER
PHOTO-ILLUSTRATION: RUSSELL PIERCE
DESIGN FIRM: VISION STREET WEAR (IN-HOUSE)
CLIENT: VISION STREET WEAR
COUNTRY: USA

CREATIVE DIRECTOR/DESIGNER/ILLUSTRATOR: RUSSELL PIERCE
PHOTOGRAPHER: MARTIN BROWER
PHOTO-ILLUSTRATION: RUSSELL PIERCE
DESIGN FIRM: VISION STREET WEAR (IN-HOUSE)
CLIENT: VISION STREET WEAR
COUNTRY: USA

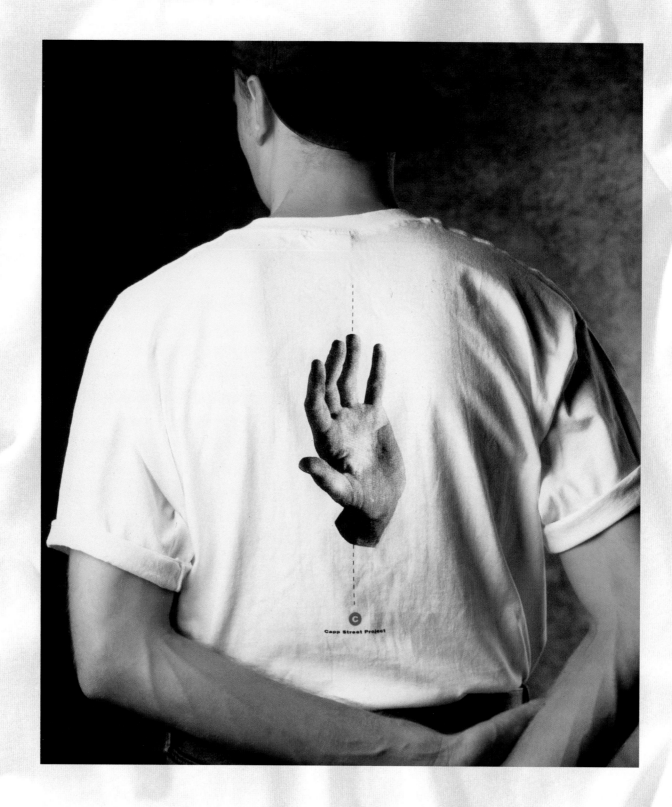

ART DIRECTOR: JENNIFER MORLA
DESIGNERS: JENNIFER MORLA, SHARRIE BROOKS
PHOTOGRAPHER: HOLLY STEWART
MODEL: CRAIG BAILEY
DESIGN FIRM: MORLA DESIGN
CLIENT: CAPP STREET PROJECT
COUNTRY: USA

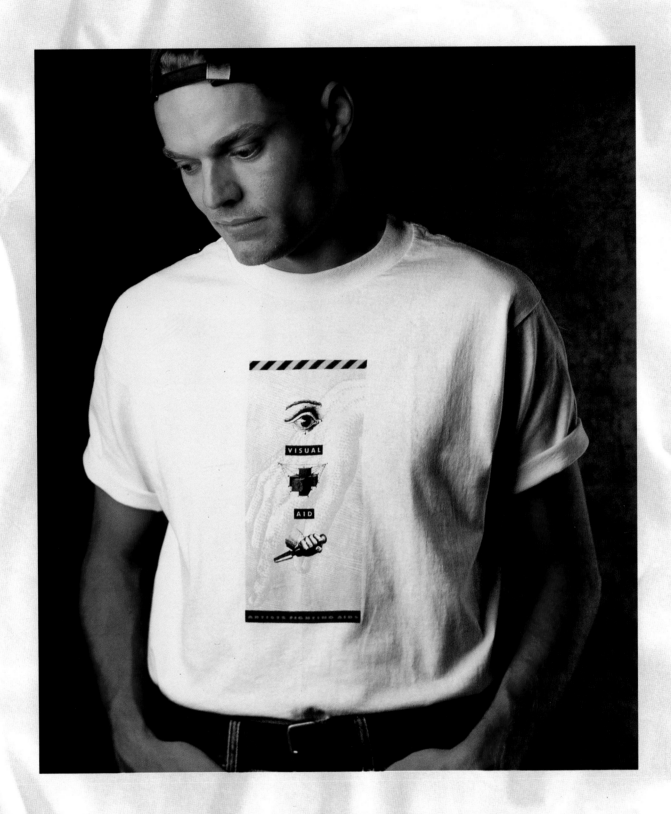

ART DIRECTOR: JENNIFER MORLA
DESIGNERS: JENNIFER MORLA, SHARRIE BROOKS
PHOTOGRAPHER: HOLLY STEWART
MODEL: CRAIG BAILEY
DESIGN FIRM: MORLA DESIGN
CLIENT: VISUAL AID
COUNTRY: USA

ART DIRECTOR/DESIGNER: PIERRE-EMMANUEL MEUNIER

PHOTOGRAPHER: PIERRE-EMMANUEL MEUNIER

MODEL: BRUNO

DESIGN FIRM: PETER LOVES

COUNTRY: FRANCE

ART DIRECTOR/DESIGNER: PIERRE-EMMANUEL MEUNIER
PHOTOGRAPHER: PIERRE-EMMANUEL MEUNIER
MODEL: JERRY
DESIGN FIRM: PETER LOVES
COUNTRY: FRANCE

russell pierce

CREATIVE DIRECTOR/DESIGNER/ILLUSTRATOR: RUSSELL PIERCE
PHOTOGRAPHER: MARTIN BROWER
PHOTO-ILLUSTRATION: RUSSELL PIERCE
DESIGN FIRM: VISION STREET WEAR (IN-HOUSE)
CLIENT: VISION STREET WEAR
COUNTRY: USA

CREATIVE DIRECTOR/DESIGNER/ILLUSTRATOR: RUSSELL PIERCE

PHOTOGRAPHER: MARTIN BROWER

PHOTO-ILLUSTRATION: RUSSELL PIERCE

DESIGN FIRM: VISION STREET WEAR (IN-HOUSE)

CLIENT: MTV

COUNTRY: USA

First Step

■ (OPPOSITE PAGE) Art Director/Designer: KRISTIN SOMMESE Photographer: KRISTIN SOMMESE Models: KAITLIN, BOBBY Design Firm: SOMMESE DESIGN Client: SY BARASH REGATTA/AMERICAN CANCER SOCIETY Country: USA ■ (THIS PAGE) Art Director: LANA RIGSBY Designer: LANA RIGSBY Illustrator: LANA RIGSBY Photographer: SANDY KING Model: KATY Design Firm: RIGSBY DESIGN, INC. Client: FIRST STEP Country: USA

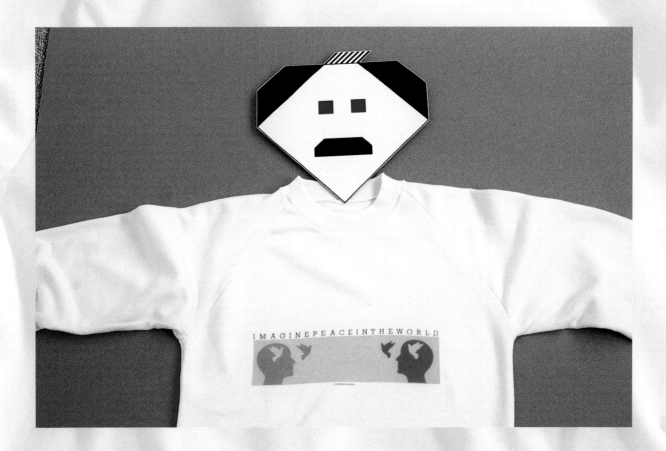

■ (PRECEEDING SPREAD) Art Director: RIK ZAK Designer: RIK ZAK Illustrators: CHRIS ARMSTRONG (PAGE 158), DAVE CARSON (PAGE 159) Photographer: GERARD YUNKER Stylist: PATRICK TRUDEAU Model: KYLE/STREIT MODEL MANAGEMENT Design Firm: SENSETIVE IN4MATION INC. Client: REZIST Country: CANADA ■ (OPPOSITE PAGE) Art Director: DONALD L. KIEL Designer: DONALD L. KIEL Photographer: MARY A. KELLY Design Firm: SWANKE HAYDEN CONNELL ARCHITECTS Client: THE INSTITUTE OF BUSINESS DESIGNERS NEW YORK CHAPTER Country: USA ■ (THIS PAGE) Art Director: FERNANDO MEDINA Designer: FERNANDO MEDINA Illustrator: FERNANDO MEDINA Photography: TRIOM DESIGN Design Firm/Client: TRIOM DESIGN Country: USA

ART DIRECTOR/DESIGNER: SCOTT THARES
PHOTOGRAPHER: PAUL IRMITER
DESIGN FIRM/CLIENT: JOHN RYAN COMPANY
COUNTRY: USA

ART DIRECTOR/DESIGNER: SCOTT THARES
PHOTOGRAPHER: PAUL IRMITER
DESIGN FIRM/CLIENT: JOHN RYAN COMPANY
COUNTRY: USA

ART DIRECTOR: ROBERT LEAR
DESIGNER: LINDA CARTE
ILLUSTRATOR: ANSON LIAW
PHOTOGRAPHER: ROBERT LEAR
MODEL: ANSON LIAW
CLIENT: KENYA WILDLIFE FUND
COUNTRY: USA

ART DIRECTOR/DESIGNER: LANA RIGSBY
ILLUSTRATOR: TROY FORD
PHOTOGRAPHER: ARTHUR MEYERSON
MODELS: JESSICA, DYLAN, KATIE, JACOB, ALLISON
DESIGN FIRM: LOWELL WILLIAMS DESIGN
CLIENT: THE ZOOLOGICAL SOCIETY OF HOUSTON
COUNTRY: USA

drogen!

Eine Initiative von
Rudolf & Spörrer Design
und Art Concepts

■ (OPPOSITE PAGE) ART DIRECTOR/DESIGNER: PIERRE MENDELL PHOTOGRAPHER: KLAUS OBERER MODEL: ASLAN HUGHES DESIGN FIRM: MENDELL & OBERER CLIENT: MENDELL & OBERER COUNTRY: GERMANY ■ (THIS PAGE) ART DIRECTOR/PHOTOGRAPHER: PAUL KALKBRENNER DESIGNER: ROLF LEUKEL MODEL: SABINE DESIGN FIRM: ABGANG! CLIENT: ABGANG! COUNTRY: GERMANY ■ (FOLLOWING SPREAD, LEFT) ART DIRECTOR/DESIGNER/ILLUSTRATOR: LYNN RIDDLE WALLER DESIGN FIRM: CLIFFORD SELBERT DESIGN CLIENT: AMNESTY INTERNATIONAL USA COUNTRY: USA ■ (FOLLOWING SPREAD, RIGHT) ART DIRECTOR: MIKEL HORL DESIGNER: PETER WOOD PHOTOGRAPHER: STUART REDLER DESIGN FIRM: THE HORLWOOD CORP. CLIENT: CONDOMANIA COUNTRY: GREAT BRITAIN

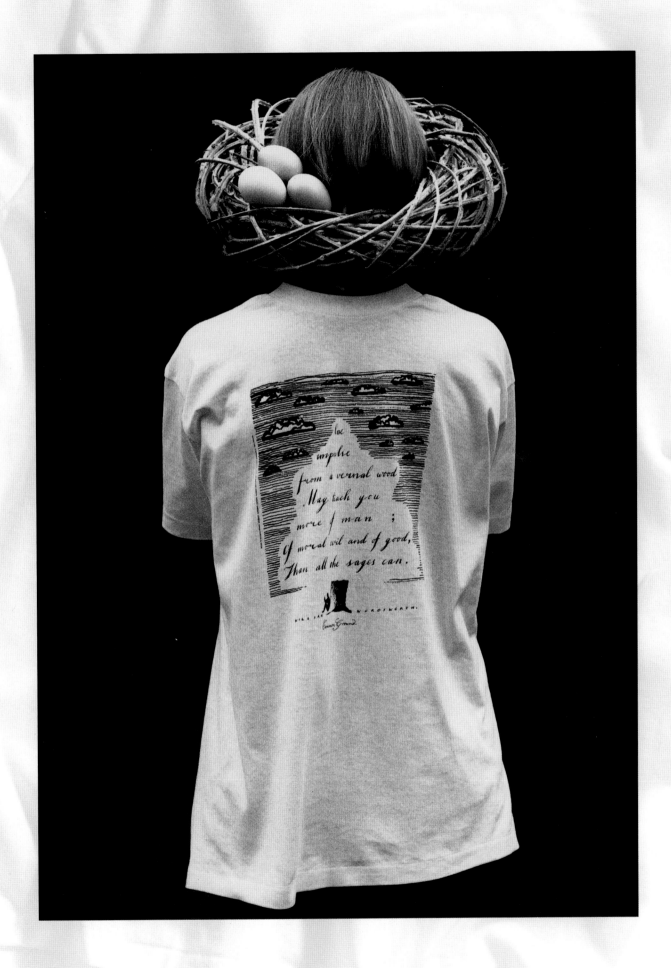

ART DIRECTOR: PAUL KALKBRENNER
DESIGNER: ROLF LEUKEL/RAUSCH
PHOTOGRAPHERS: PAUL KALKBRENNER, DETLEF SZILLAT
MODELS: MEMBERS OF THE COLOGNE BICYCLE MESSENGER SERVICE RAPIDO (OPPOSITE TOP),
PLAYERS OF THE COLOGNE CROCODILES SOCCER TEAM (OPPOSITE BOTTOM), BOY GEORGE (ABOVE)
DESIGN FIRM/CLIENT: ABGANG!
COUNTRY: GERMANY

■ (ABOVE) ART DIRECTORS/DESIGNERS: THOMAS STARR, LISA ASHWORTH, JEANNE KIM, JENNIFER BERNSTEIN, AMY GOODWIN, DIANA CADWALLADER JULI WHITNEY, DAVID PELLETIER PHOTOGRAPHER: THOMAS STARR DESIGN FIRM/CLIENT: COALITION TO FREE RU 486 COUNTRY: USA ■ (OPPOSITE PAGE) ART DIRECTOR/DESIGNER/ PHOTOGRAPHER: PIERRE-EMMANUEL MEUNIER MODEL: CÉLINE DESIGN FIRM: PETER LOVES COUNTRY: FRANCE

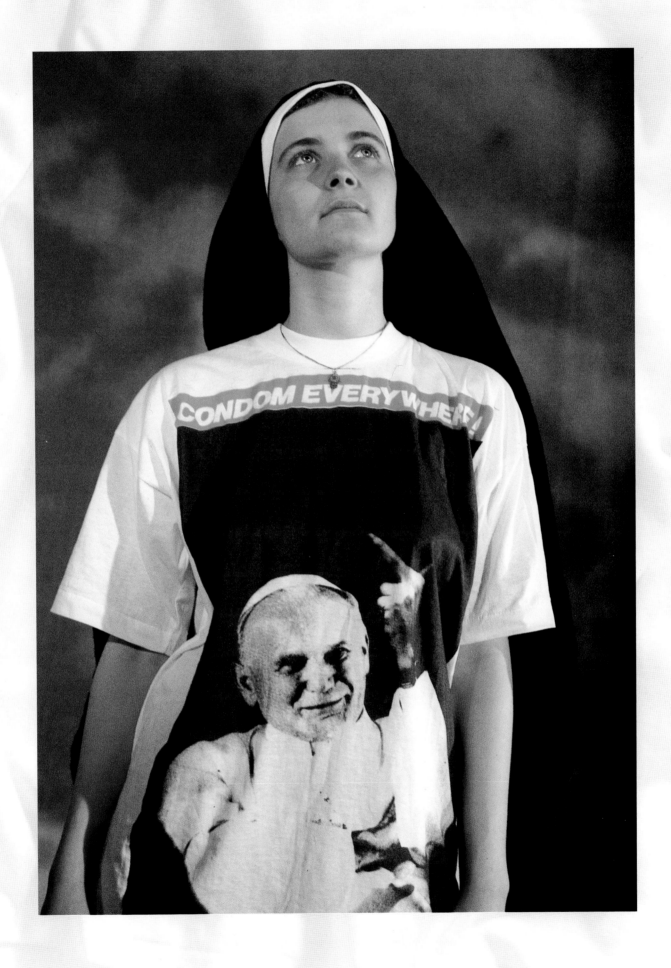

ART DIRECTOR/DESIGNER/ILLUSTRATOR/MODEL MAKER: PAUL MINETT
PHOTOGRAPHER: MARK GATEHOUSE
DESIGN FIRM: BRILLS
CLIENT: THE BIG ISSUE
COUNTRY: GREAT BRITAIN

ART DIRECTOR/DESIGNER: PAUL KALKBRENNER
PHOTOGRAPHER: PAUL KALKBRENNER
MODEL: HOLGER FEY
DESIGN FIRM/CLIENT: ABGANG!
COUNTRY: GERMANY

■ (OPPOSITE TOP) ART DIRECTOR/DESIGNER: PAUL KALKBRENNER PHOTOGRAPHER: PAUL KALKBRENNER MODEL: LILI VOIGT DESIGN FIRM/CLIENT: ABGANG! COUNTRY: GERMANY ■ (OPPOSITE BOTTOM) ART DIRECTOR/DESIGNER: PIERRE-EMMANUEL MEUNIER PHOTOGRAPHER: PIERRE-EMMANUEL MEUNIER MODEL: PIERRE-EMMANUEL MEUNIER DESIGN FIRM: PETER LOVES COUNTRY: FRANCE ■ (THIS PAGE) ART DIRECTOR/DESIGNER: PAUL KALKBRENNER PHOTOGRAPHER: PAUL KALKBRENNER MODEL: GUIDO, FRANK DESIGN FIRM/CLIENT: ABGANG! COUNTRY: GERMANY

ART DIRECTOR/DESIGNER: LESLIE A. SEGAL

PHOTOGRAPHER: LEONARD NONES

MODEL: LESLIE A. SEGAL

CLIENT: CAST IRON SEAT COLLECTORS ASSOCIATION

COUNTRY: USA

ART DIRECTOR/DESIGNER/ILLUSTRATOR: NATHALIE CUSSON
PHOTOGRAPHER: SKIP DEAN
MODEL: NATHALIE CUSSON
DESIGN FIRM: THE BULLDOG GROUP
CLIENT: SECOND HARVEST
COUNTRY: CANADA

ART DIRECTOR: RON SULLIVAN
DESIGNER: KELLY ALLEN
DESIGN FIRM: SULLIVAN PERKINS
CLIENT: MELTZER & MARTIN
COUNTRY: USA

ART DIRECTOR: RON SULLIVAN
DESIGNER: KELLY ALLEN
DESIGN FIRM: SULLIVAN PERKINS
CLIENT: MELTZER & MARTIN
COUNTRY: USA

ART DIRECTOR/DESIGNER/ILLUSTRATOR: ELKE KERN
PHOTOGRAPHER: KAI-UWE SCHNEIDER
MODEL: CLAUDIUS MAYERHÖFER
DESIGN FIRM: PUNKT KOMMA STRICH
CLIENT: MINISTERIUM FÜR ARBEIT, GESUNDHEIT UND SOZIALORDNUNG, STUTTGART
COUNTRY: GERMANY

ART DIRECTOR/DESIGNER: PAUL KOELEMAN
PHOTOGRAPHER: COR VAN GASTEL
DESIGN FIRM: STUDIO PAUL KOELEMAN
CLIENT: GAY & LESBIAN SWITCHBOARD
COUNTRY: NETHERLANDS

■ (ABOVE LEFT) ART DIRECTOR: RON SULLIVAN DESIGNER: KELLY ALLEN DESIGN FIRM: SULLIVAN PERKINS CLIENT: MENTAL HEALTH ASSOCIATION OF GREATER DALLAS COUNTRY: USA ■ (ABOVE RIGHT AND OPPOSITE PAGE) ART DIRECTOR/DESIGER: LANNY SOMMESE ILLUSTRATOR: LANNY SOMMESE PHOTOGRAPHER: KRISTIN SOMMESE DESIGN FIRM: SOMMESE DESIGN CLIENT: CENTRAL PENNSYLVANIA FESTIVAL OF THE ARTS COUNTRY: USA

ART DIRECTOR/DESIGNER/ILLUSTRATOR: CATHLEEN CHOU

PHOTOGRAPHER: MARK O. BENJAMIN

MODEL: CATHLEEN CHOU

DESIGN STUDIO: DEPT. INSTRUCTIONAL DESIGN & EVALUATION

CLIENT: NATIONAL TECHNICAL INSTITUTE FOR THE DEAF

COUNTRY: USA

ART DIRECTOR/DESIGNER/ILLUSTRATOR: MARIE BUCKLEY

PHOTOGRAPHER: MARK O. BENJAMIN

MODEL: MARIE BUCKLEY

DESIGN STUDIO: DEPT. INSTRUCTIONAL DESIGN & EVALUATION

CLIENT: NATIONAL TECHNICAL INSTITUTE FOR THE DEAF

COUNTRY: USA

■ (OPPOSITE TOP) Art Director/Designer/Photographer: PIERRE-EMMANUEL MEUNIER Models: ISABELLE, JERRY Design Firm: PETER LOVES Country: FRANCE ■ (OPPOSITE BOTTOM) Art Director/Designer/Illustrator: TODD COATS Photographer: CHUCK CARLTON Model: TODD COATS Design Firm: TODD COATS DESIGN Client: AIDS AWARENESS Country: USA ■ (THIS PAGE) Art Director: JAN VAN DER LEE Illustrator/Model: NICOLETTE WEVER Photographer: JAN WILLEM SCHOLTEN Design Firm: THE REP'S Client: ANIMAL SUPPORT Country: NETHERLANDS

ART DIRECTOR/DESIGNER: PAUL KOELEMAN
PHOTOGRAPHER: COR VAN GASTEL
DESIGN FIRM: STUDIO PAUL KOELEMAN
CLIENT: HET NATIONALE BALLET
COUNTRY: NETHERLANDS

ART DIRECTOR/DESIGNER/ILLUSTRATOR/PHOTOGRAPHER: JELENA KITAJEVA
MODELS: STARS OF THE BYELORUSSIAN BALLET
DESIGN FIRM: JELENA KITAJEVA
CLIENT: ACADEMIC BOLSHOJ BALLET THEATRE
COUNTRY: WHITERUSSIA

 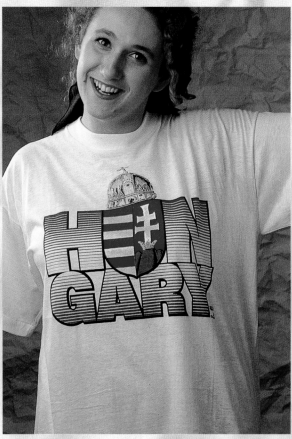

■ (PRECEEDING SPREAD) Art Director/Designer: CARLA RUMLER Photographer: ANDREAS SMETANA Design Firm/Client: TIROL WERBUNG Country: AUSTRIA ■ (THIS PAGE, LEFT) Art Director/Designer: BORIS LJUBICIC Photographer: RAJNA BUZIC-LJUBICIC Design Firm: STUDIO INTERNATIONAL Client: CROATIA BATERIES Country: CROATIA ■ (THIS PAGE, RIGHT) Art Director/Designer: DRAGUTIN DADO KOVACEVIC Photographer: FJODOR FATICIC Design Firm: DESIGN ART Client: ART-SHIRT Country: CROATIA ■ (OPPOSITE PAGE) Designer/Model: RUTH ADLER DAYAN Photographer: SHLUMITE LAVI Client: LIPTI Country: ISRAEL

■ (THIS PAGE, LEFT) ART DIRECTOR: MIA SWOBODA DESIGNER/ILLUSTRATOR: CHRISTIAN PREUSCHL-HALDENBURG
PHOTOGRAPHER: ELISABETH STRAUSS MODEL: DANIEL COUNTRY: AUSTRIA ■ (THIS PAGE, RIGHT, AND OPPOSITE)
ART DIRECTOR: DRAGUTIN DADO KOVACEVIC DESIGNER: DRAGUTIN DADO KOVACEVIC HAND PAINTING: DRAGUTIN
DADO KOVACEVIC PHOTOGRAPHER: FJODOR FATICIC DESIGN FIRM: DESIGN ART COUNTRY: CROATIA

■ (OPPOSITE PAGE) 1, 2, 7 DESIGNER: JOE MILLER PHOTOGRAPHER: GLENN MATSUMURA DESIGN FIRM: JOE MILLER'S COMPANY CLIENT: KSJS PUBLIC RADIO COUNTRY: USA ■ 3 ART DIRECTOR/DESIGNER/ILLUSTRATOR: WILLIAM HOMAN DESIGN FIRM/CLIENT: JOHN RYAN CO. COUNTRY: USA ■ 4 ART DIRECTOR: HOLLY RUSSELL DESIGNER/ILLUSTRATOR: PAUL BARTH PHOTOGRAPHER: GREG PLACHTA DESIGN FIRM: GLAXO CORPORATE CREATIVE SERVICES CLIENT: GLAXO 1993 EXECUTIVE CONFERENCE COUNTRY: USA ■ 5 ART DIRECTOR: JOHN HORNALL DESIGNERS: JOHN HORNALL, MIKE COURTNEY, BRIAN O'NEILL, DAVID BATES DESIGN FIRM: HORNALL ANDERSON DESIGN WORKS CLIENT: SEATTLE ART MUSEUM COUNTRY: USA ■ 6 ART DIRECTOR/DESIGNER: RICHARD BIRD ILLUSTRATOR: RENEE GONZALEZ PHOTOGRAPHER: JOSEPH FAVATA MODEL: RENEE GONZALEZ DESIGN FIRM: R. BIRD & COMPANY CLIENT: INTERNATIONAL CONSULTANTS OF THE ENVIRONMENT COUNTRY: USA ■ 8 DESIGNER: JOE MILLER PHOTOGRAPHER: GLENN MATSUMURA DESIGN FIRM: JOE MILLER'S COMPANY CLIENT: WORKS GALLERY COUNTRY: USA ■ (THIS PAGE) DESIGNERS: PAUL KALKBRENNER, MICHAEL HOOYMANN PHOTOGRAPHER: PAUL KALKBRENNER MODEL: CHRISTIAN KALINOWSKI DESIGN FIRM: ABGANG! CLIENT: ABGANG! COUNTRY: GERMANY

■ (THIS PAGE) Art Directors: STAVROS VIDALIS, FRÉDÉRIC GRAF Designer/Illustrator: JACKY GUILARTE
Photographer: STAVROS VIDALIS Model: LAURENT VAUCLAIR Client: INDIGO FASHION PRINT Country: SWITZER-
LAND ■ (OPPOSITE PAGE) 1, 2 Designer/Model: DOMINIK LAHAYE Photographer: HEINZ-PETER LAHAYE Country:
GERMANY ■ 3 Designer: MELA ROSENKIND Photographer: CLAUDIA PÖRSCH Models: MELA AND MICKY
ROSENKIND Country: GERMANY ■ 4 Art Director: PETER KRINNINGER Designer: MAX LOCHNER Photographer:
PETER KRINNINGER Model: VERENA Client: MAX MAD HOUSE Country: GERMANY ■ 5, 8 Art Director/Designer:
DRAGUTIN DADO KOVACEVIC Photographer: FJODOR FATICIC Design Firm: DESIGN ART Country: CROATIA ■ 6
Designer/Illustrator/Photographer: GABOR FEKETE Model: SUSAN HENGGELER Client: T-SHIRT-ART LUZERN
Country: SWITZERLAND ■ 7 Art Directors: MARKUS KRIPS, PAUL KALKBRENNER Designer: MARKUS KRIPS
Photographer: PAUL KALKBRENNER Model: ROLAND FRANKEN Design Firm/Client: ABGANG! Country: GERMANY

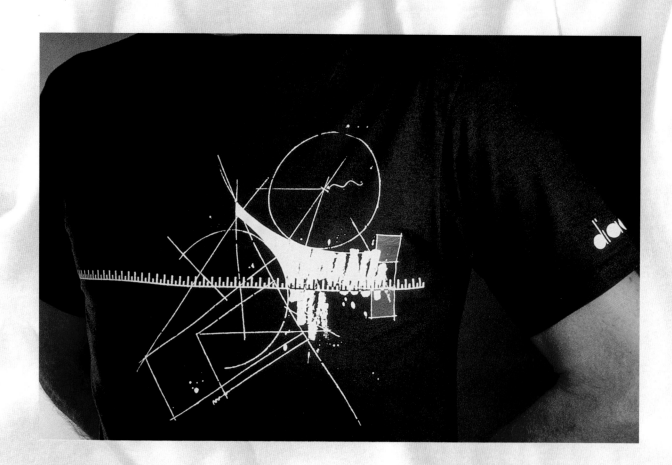

■ (THIS PAGE) ART DIRECTOR/ILLUSTRATOR: JACK ANDERSON DESIGNERS: JACK ANDERSON, CHERI HUBER DESIGN FIRM: HORNALL ANDERSON DESIGN WORKS CLIENT: DIADORA AMERICA COUNTRY: USA ■ (OPPOSITE PAGE) 1 ART DIRECTOR: JULIANE SCHLAEFKE PHOTOGRAPHER: CARSTEN HEIDMANN/"LOGO", BREMEN MODELS: LIANGZHI CHENG, NICOLE SCHUBERT DESIGN FIRM/CLIENT: TRIO BREMEN COUNTRY: GERMANY ■ 2 DESIGNER: ALEXANDER STROHMAIER PHOTOGRAPHER: STEFAN JETTER MODEL: SUMITRA NANJUNDAN COUNTRY: AUSTRIA ■ 3, 4 ART DIRECTOR/DESIGNER/ILLUSTRATOR/PHOTOGRAPHER/CLIENT: GYÖRGY KEMÉNY COUNTRY: HUNGARY ■ 5 ART DIRECTOR/DESIGNER: ALFRED LACHER PHOTOGRAPHER: MAXIMILIAN LACHER MODEL: MONIKA FEICHTINGER CLIENT: CHRISTIAN SCHMITZ COUNTRY: AUSTRIA

■ (THIS PAGE) DESIGNER: M. SCHINGERLIN PHOTOGRAPHER: FRANCOIS SWANEPOEL DESIGN FIRM: M. SCHINGERLIN
CLIENT: OUT OF AFRICA COUNTRY: SOUTH AFRICA ■ (OPPOSITE PAGE) 1, 3 ART DIRECTOR/DESIGNER/ILLUSTRATOR:
RUSSEL HALFHIDE PHOTOGRAPHER: MARK LYNDERSAY DESIGN FIRM: RUSSEL HALFHIDE CLIENT: CROLON LIFE
CARIBBEAN LTD. (1), PAN TRINBAGO (3) COUNTRY: WEST INDIES ■ 2, 4 ART DIRECTION/DESIGN/ILLUSTRATION/DESIGN
FIRM/CLIENT: : T-SHIRT-KLUB PHOTOGRAPHER: KNUT GROEGER MODELS: MEMBERS OF THE "T-SHIRT-KLUB" COUNTRY:
GERMANY ■ 5 ART DIRECTOR/DESIGNER/ILLUSTRATOR: HEINO PRUNSVELT PHOTOGRAPHER: BORIS MÄEMETS MODEL: RIINA
DESIGN FIRM: VAAL DESIGN CLIENT: COMMITTEE OF EAST-WEST UNITED SONG FESTIVAL '91 COUNTRY: ESTONIA ■ 6
ART DIRECTOR/DESIGNER: DENNIS EDGE PHOTOGRAPHER: LOIS CARLO MODEL: DENNIS EDGE DESIGN FIRM: DENNIS EDGE
DESIGN CLIENT: PUBLIC AWARENESS CAMPAIGN COUNTRY: USA ■ 7 ART DIRECTOR/DESIGNER/ILLUSTRATOR: JOHN EVANS
PHOTOGRAPHER: STEVE WOODS MODEL: BONNIE FISH DESIGN FIRM: JOHN EVANS DESIGN PRINTER: ADRIAN RAY
COUNTRY: USA ■ 8 ART DIRECTOR: THOMAS FRIK PHOTOGRAPHER: LUIS STEINKELLNER MODEL: NEAL VINCENT DESIGN
FIRM: WASSAK & FRIK CLIENT: LUIS STEINKELLNER COUNTRY: AUSTRIA ■ 9 ART DIRECTOR/DESIGNER/ILLUSTRATOR:
DRAGUTIN DADO KOVACEVIC PHOTOGRAPHER: FJODOR FATICIC DESIGN FIRM: DESIGN ART COUNTRY: CROATIA

■ (OPPOSITE PAGE): **1** ART DIRECTOR/DESIGNER: BORIS LJUBICIC PHOTOGRAPHER: RAJNA BUZIC-LJUBICIC DESIGN FIRM: STUDIO INTERNATIONAL CLIENT: EKONERG COUNTRY: CROATIA ■ **2** ART DIRECTOR/DESIGNER: VICTOR GOYTIA PHOTOGRAPHER: JOSE DE JESUS QUESADA CLIENT: JAVIER SANTOS COUNTRY: MEXICO ■ **3** ART DIRECTOR/ILLUSTRA-TOR/PHOTOGRAPHER: KEITH HARRIS DESIGNERS: KEITH HARRIS, ULRIKE HARNAU MODEL: LINDA CHUNG CLIENT: CASSIE EISKREM GMBH COUNTRY: GERMANY ■ **4** ART DIRECTOR/DESIGNER: ELEANOR ADAM ILLUSTRATOR: ELEANOR ADAM PHOTOGRAPHER: JOHN SCHWARTZ MODEL: JAMIE COLUMBUS COUNTRY: USA ■ **5** ART DIRECTOR/DESIGNER: SEPPO SAVOLAINEN MODEL: TEVA GLAD DESIGN FIRM: ACTION DIRECT OY CLIENT: RADIO FINLANDIA, MARBELLA COUNTRY: SPAIN ■ **6** ART DIRECTOR: JOSE SERRANO ILLUSTRATOR: DAN THONER PHOTOGRAPHER: CARL VANDERSCHUIT MODEL: JANE SPOTTE DESIGN FIRM: MIRES DESIGN, INC. CLIENT: TEE-SHIRT CO. COUNTRY: USA ■ **7** ILLUSTRATOR: GITTA WITZKE PHOTOGRAPHER: PETRA SCHONNEFELD MODEL: EVA HOFFS DESIGN FIRM: Z-ART CLIENT: ELECTROLA COUNTRY: GERMANY ■ **8** ART DIRECTOR/DESIGNER: MERVIL M. PAYLOR ILLUSTRATOR: MERVIL M. PAYLOR PHOTOGRAPHER: RON CHAPPLE 1DESIGN FIRM: MERVIL PAYLOR DESIGN CLIENT: RON CHAPPLE PHOTOGRAPHY COUNTRY: USA ■ **9** ART DIRECTOR/DESIGNER/ILLUSTRATOR: PATRICK SHORT PHOTOGRAPHER: TODD MCLEOD MODEL: FAITH MURPHY DESIGN FIRM: BLACKBIRD DESIGN CLIENT: THE BEACHED WHALE CAFE COUNTRY: USA ■ (THIS PAGE) ART DIRECTOR/DESIGNER/ILLUSTRATOR: FRANK XAVER HAUSMANN PHOTOGRAPHER: HUBERT CZECH DESIGN FIRM: FXH GRAPHIC-ART-DESIGN STUDIO CLIENT: CLASSIC CAR SERVICE COUNTRY: GERMANY

ART DIRECTOR: DAVID FREEMAN
DESIGNER/ILLUSTRATOR: LEE HODDY
PHOTOGRAPHER: MARIUS VAN DER PLAS
MODEL: LORRAINE WOODVINE
DESIGN FIRM: SAMPSON TYRRELL LTD.
CLIENT: WPP GROUP PLC
COUNTRY: GREAT BRITAIN

INDEX

VERZEICHNIS

INDEX

. . . .

A R T I S T S · I L L U S T R A T O R S · P H O T O G R A P H E R S

. . . .

. . . .

DESIGN FIRMS

. . . .

CALL FOR ENTRIES

EINLADUNG

APPEL D'ENVOIS

CALL FOR ENTRIES

Graphis Poster 96 · Entry Deadline: April 30, 1995

■ Advertising, cultural, and social posters. Eligibility: All work produced between May 1994 and April 1995. ● Plakate für Werbezwecke sowie kulturelle und soziale Plakate. In Frage kommen: Arbeiten, die zwischen Mai 1994 und April 1995 entstanden sind. ▲ Affiches publicitaires, culturelles et sociales. Seront admis: tous les travaux réalisés entre mai 1994 et avril 1995.

Graphis Photo 95 · Entry Deadline: August 31, 1994

■ Ads, catalogs, invitations, announcements, record covers, and calendars on any subject.. Photographs taken for consumer or trade magazines, newspapers, books and corporate publications. Personal studies on any subject. Experimental or student work on any subject. Eligibility: All work produced between September 1993 and August 1994. ● Anzeigen, Kataloge, Plattenhüllen, Kalender. Photos für Zeitschriften, Zeitungen, Bücher und Firmenpublikationen. Persönliche Studien. Experimentelle Aufnahmen oder Studentenarbeiten. In Frage kommen: Arbeiten, die zwischen September 1993 und August 1994 entstanden sind. ▲ Publicité, catalogues, invitations, annonces, pochettes de disques, calendriers. Reportages pour magazines et journaux, livres et publications d'entreprise. Études personnelles, créations expérimentales ou projets d'étudiants. Seront admis: tous les travaux réalisés entre septembre 1993 et août 1994.

Graphis Design 96 · Entry Deadline: November 30, 1994

■ Ads; promotion brochures, catalogs, invitations, record covers, announcements, logos, corporate campaigns, calendars, books, book covers, packaging, company magazines; newspapers, consumer or trade magazines, annual reports; illustration. Eligibility: All work produced between December 1, 1993 and November 30, 1994. ● Werbung, Broschüren, Kataloge, Plattenhüllen, Logos, Firmenkampagnen, Kalender, Bücher, Buchumschläge, Packungen. Zeitschriften, Hauszeitschriften, Jahresberichte, Illustrationen. In Frage kommen: Arbeiten, die zwischen Dezember 1993 und November 1994 entstanden sind. ▲ Publicité; brochures, catalogues, invitations, pochettes de disques, annonces, logos, identité visuelle, calendriers, livres, packaging;journaux, revues, magazines de sociétés, rapports annuels; illustration. Seront admis: les travaux réalisés entre décembre 1993 et novembre 1994.

■ **What to send:** Reproduction-quality duplicate transparencies (4x5" or 35mm). They are required for large, bulky or valuable pieces. ALL 35MM SLIDES MUST BE CARDBOARD-MOUNTED, NO GLASS SLIDE MOUNTS PLEASE! *Please mark the transparencies with your name.* If you do send printed pieces they should be unmounted, but well protected. WE REGRET THAT ENTRIES CANNOT BE RETURNED. ● **Was einsenden:** Wenn immer möglich, schicken Sie uns bitte reproduktionsfähige Duplikatdias. *Bitte Dias mit Ihrem Namen versehen.* Bitte schicken Sie auf keinen Fall Originaldias. KLEINBILDDIAS BITTE IM KARTONRAHMEN, KEIN GLAS! Falls Sie uns das gedruckte Beispiel schicken, bitten wir Sie, dieses gut geschützt aber nicht aufgezogen zu senden. WIR BEDAUERN, DASS EINSENDUNGEN NICHT ZURÜCKGESCHICKT WERDEN KÖNNEN. ■ **Que nous envoyer:** Nous vous recommandons de nous faire parvenir de préférence des duplicata de diapositives (4x5" ou 35mm. N'oubliez pas d'inscrire votre nom dessus). NE PAS ENVOYER DE DIAPOSITIVES SOUS VERRE! Si vous désirez envoyer des travaux imprimés, protégez-les, mais ne les montez pas sur carton. *Nous vous signalons que les envois que vous nous aurez fait parvenir ne pourront vous être retournés.*

■ **How to package your entry:** Please tape (do not glue) the completed entry form (or a copy) to the back of each piece. Please do not send anything by air freight. Write "No Commercial Value" on the package, and label it "Art for Contest." ● **Wie und wohin senden:** Bitte befestigen Sie das ausgefüllte Einsendeetikett (oder eine Kopie davon) mit Klebstreifen (nicht kleben) auf jeder Arbeit und legen Sie noch ein Doppel davon lose bei. Bitte auf keinen Fall Luft- oder Bahnfracht senden. Deklarieren Sie «Ohne jeden Handelswert» und «Arbeitsproben für Wettbewerb». ▲ **Comment préparer votre envoi:** Veuillez scotcher (ne pas coller) au dos de chaque spécimen les étiquettes dûment remplies. Nous vous prions également de faire un double de chaque étiquette, que vous joindrez à votre envoi, mais sans le coller ou le fixer. Ne nous expédiez rien en fret aérien. Indiquez «Sans aucune valeur commerciale» et «Echantillons pour concours».

■ **Entry fees** Single entries: United States U.S. $15; Germany, DM 15,00; all other countries, SFr 15.00. Three or more pieces entered in a single contest: North America, U.S. $35, Germany DM 40,00, All other countries SFr 40.00. These entry fees do not apply to countries with exchange controls or to students (please send copy of student identification). ● **Einsendegebühren:** Für jede einzelne Arbeit: Deutschland DM 15.00, alle andern Länder SFr 15.00. Für jede Kampagne oder Serie von drei oder mehr Stück: Deutschland DM 40.00, übrige Länder SFr 40.00. Für Studenten (Ausweiskopie mitschicken) und Länder mit Devisenbeschränkugen gelten diese Einsendegebühren nicht. ▲ **Droits d'admission**: Envoi d'un seul travail: pour l'Amérique du Nord, US$ 15.00; pour tous les autres pays: SFr. 15.00. Campagne ou série de trois travaux ou plus pour un seul concours: Amérique du Nord, US$ 35.00; autres pays: SFr. 40.00. Les participants de pays qui connaissent des restrictions monétaires sont dispensés des droits d'admission, au même titre que les étudiants (veuillez envoyer une photocopie de la carte d'étudiant).

■ **Where to send:** Entries from the United States and Canada should be sent to the New York office and checks should be made payable to GRAPHIS US, INC, NEW YORK. Entries from all other countries should be sent to the Zurich office and checks should be made payable to GRAPHIS PRESS CORP., ZURICH. ● **Wohin senden:** Bitte senden Sie uns Ihre Arbeiten an Graphis Zürich zusammen mit einem Scheck, ausgestellt in SFr. (auf eine Schweizer Bank ziehen oder Eurocheck) oder überweisen Sie den Betrag auf PC Luzern 60-3520-6 oder PSchK Frankfurt 3000 57-602 (BLZ 50010060). ▲ **Où envoyer:** Veuillez envoyer vos travaux à Graphis Zurich et joindre un chèque tiré sur une banque suisse ou un Eurochèque; ou verser le montant sur le compte chèque postal Lucerne 60–3520–6.

Graphis Press, Dufourstrasse 107, CH-8008 Zürich, Switzerland, telephone: 41-1-383 82 11, fax: 41-1-383 16 43
Graphis US, Inc., 141 Lexington Avenue, New York, NY 10016, telephone: (212) 532 9387, fax: (212) 213 3229

E N T R Y   F O R M

I wish to enter the attached in the following Graphis competition:

. . . .

☐ **GRAPHIS POSTER 96**

(APRIL 30, 1995)

CATEGORY CODES/KATEGORIEN/CATÉGORIES

PO1 ADVERTISING/WERBUNG/PUBLICITÉ

PO2 PROMOTION

PO3 CULTURE/KULTUR

PO4 SOCIAL/GESELLSCHAFT/SOCIÉTÉ

☐ **GRAPHIS PHOTO 95**

(AUGUST 31, 1994)

CATEGORY CODES/KATEGORIEN/CATÉGORIES

PH1 FASHION/MODE

PH2 JOURNALISM/JOURNALISMUS

PH3 STILL LIFE/STILLEBEN/NATURE MORTE

PH4 FOOD/LEBENSMITTEL/CUISINE

PH5 PEOPLE/MENSCHEN/PERSONNES

PH6 PRODUCTS/PRODUKTE/PRODUITS

PH7 LANDSCAPES/LANDSCHAFTEN/EXTÉRIEURS

PH8 ARCHITECTURE/ARCHITEKTUR

PH9 WILD LIFE/TIERE/ANIMAUX

PH10 SPORTS/SPORT

PH11 FINE ART/KUNST/ART

☐ **GRAPHIS DESIGN 96**

(NOVEMBER 30, 1994)

CATEGORY CODES/KATEGORIEN/CATÉGORIES

DE1 ADVERTISING/WERBUNG/ PUBLICITÉ

DE2 BOOKS/BÜCHER/LIVRES

DE3 BROCHURES/BROSCHÜREN

DE4 CALENDARS/KALENDER/CALENDRIERS

DE5 CORPORATE IDENTITY

DE6 EDITORIAL/REDAKTIONELL/RÉDACTIONNEL

DE7 ILLUSTRATION

DE8 PACKAGING/VERPACKUNG

DE9 MISCELLANEOUS/ANDERE/DIVERS

TAPE (DON'T GLUE) A COMPLETED COPY OF THIS FORM TO THE BACK OF EACH ENTRY

BITTE AUF DER RÜCKSEITE JEDER ARBEIT MIT KLEBBAND BEFESTIGEN
VEUILLEZ SCOTCHER (NE PAS COLLER) AU DOS DE CHAQUE ENVOI

TITLE OF ENTRY

TITEL DER ARBEIT
TITRE DE L'ENVOI

CATEGORY CODE   **YEAR CREATED/PUBLISHED**

KATEGORIENCODE   **ENTSTANDEN/PUBLIZIERT**
CODE DE CATÉGORIE   **CRÉÉ/PUBLIÉ (ANNÉE)**

PERSON/COMPANY ENTERING WORK

PRINT NAME

NAME DES EINSENDERS
TRAVAIL ENVOYÉ PAR

TITLE

COMPANY

TITEL/TITRE

ADDRESS

FIRMA/SOCIÉTÉ

CITY/ZIP

ADRESSE

STATE   **COUNTRY**

PLZ/STADT/LAND
VILLE/CODE POSTAL/PAYS

TELEPHONE   **FAX**

TELEPHON   **FAX**

Ich erteile Graphis hiermit das Recht zur unentgeltlichen Veröffentlichung meiner Arbeit in den Graphis-Publikationen sowie in Anzeigen oder Broschüren zu Werbezwecken der Graphis-Publikationen.

I hereby grant permission for the attached material to be published free of charge in any Graphis book, article in *Graphis* magazine, or any advertisement, brochure or other material produced for the purpose of promoting Graphis publications.

Par la présente, j'autorise les Editions Graphis à publier le travail ci-joint à titre gracieux dans tout livre Graphis, dans tout article du magazine *Graphis*, ainsi que tout matériel publicitaire, brochure, dépliant ou autre, destiné à la promotion des publication Graphis.

SIGNATURE   **DATE**

DATUM   **UNTERSCHRIFT**
DATE   **SIGNATURE**

Mail entries to:

Graphis Press, Dufourstrasse 107, CH-8008 Zürich, or
Graphis US, Inc., 141 Lexington Ave, New York, NY 10016

Bitte senden Sie Ihre Arbeit an/Veuillez envoyer à l'adresse suivante::

Graphis Verlag AG, Dufourstrasse 107, CH-8008 Zürich,
Schweiz, Telephon: 01-383-82-11, Telefax: 01-383-16-43

G R A P H I S B O O K S

BOOKS	ALL REGIONS
☐ GRAPHIS DESIGN 94	US$ 69.00
☐ GRAPHIS PHOTO 93	US$ 69.00
☐ GRAPHIS poster 94	US$ 69.00
☐ GRAPHIS LETTERHEAD 2	US$ 69.00
☐ GRAPHIS LOGO 2	US$ 60.00
☐ GRAPHIS TYPOGRAPHY 1	US$ 75.00
☐ GRAPHIS NUDES	US$ 85.00
☐ GRAPHIS ANNUAL REPORTS 4	US$ 75.00
☐ GRAPHIS CORPORATE IDENTITY 2	US$ 75.00
☐ ROCK SCISSORS PAPER	US$195.00
☐ GRAPHIS PUBLICATION 1 (ENGLISH)	US$ 75.00
☐ ART FOR SURVIVAL: THE ILLUSTRATOR AND THE ENVIRONMENT	US$ 45.00

☐ CHECK ENCLOSED (PAYABLE TO GRAPHIS)
  (US$ ONLY, DRAWN ON A BANK IN THE USA)

USE CREDIT CARDS (DEBITED IN US DOLLARS)

☐ AMERICAN EXPRESS   ☐ MASTERCARD   ☐ VISA

CARD NO.   EXP. DATE

CARDHOLDER NAME

SIGNATURE

☐ PLEASE BILL ME (BOOK(S) WILL BE SENT WHEN PAYMENT IS
  RECEIVED)

(PLEASE PRINT)

NAME

TITLE

COMPANY

ADDRESS

CITY

STATE/PROVINCE   ZIP CODE

COUNTRY

SEND ORDER FORM AND MAKE CHECK PAYABLE TO:
GRAPHIS US, INC.,
141 LEXINGTON AVENUE,
NEW YORK, NY 10016-8193, USA

REQUEST FOR CALL FOR ENTRIES
PLEASE PUT ME ON YOUR "CALL FOR ENTRIES" LIST FOR THE
FOLLOWING TITLES:

☐ GRAPHIS DESIGN   ☐ GRAPHIS ANNUAL REPORTS
☐ GRAPHIS DIAGRAM   ☐ GRAPHIS CORPORATE IDENTITY
☐ GRAPHIS POSTER   ☐ GRAPHIS PACKAGING
☐ GRAPHIS PHOTO   ☐ GRAPHIS LETTERHEAD
☐ GRAPHIS LOGO   ☐ GRAPHIS TYPOGRAPHY

SUBMITTING MATERIAL TO ANY OF THE ABOVE TITLES QUALIFIES
SENDER FOR A DISCOUNT TOWARDS PURCHASE OF THAT TITLE.

BOOKS	EUROPE/AFRICA MIDDLE EAST	GERMANY	U.K.
☐ GRAPHIS DESIGN 94	SFR.123.–	DM 149,–	£ 52.00
☐ GRAPHIS PHOTO 93	SFR.123.–	DM 149,–	£ 52.00
☐ GRAPHIS POSTER 94	SFR.123.–	DM 149,–	£ 52.00
☐ GRAPHIS LETTERHEAD 2	SFR.123.–	DM 149,–	£ 52.00
☐ GRAPHIS LOGO 2	SFR. 92.–	DM 108,–	£ 38.00
☐ GRAPHIS TYPOGRAPHY 1	SFR.137.–	DM 162,–	£ 55.00
☐ GRAPHIS NUDES	SFR.168.–	DM 168,–	£ 62.00
☐ ANNUAL REPORTS 4	SFR.137.–	DM 162,–	£ 55.00
☐ CORPORATE IDENTITY 2	SFR.137.–	DM 162,–	£ 55.00
☐ GRAPHIS PUBLICATION 1			
☐ ENGLISH ☐ GERMAN	SFR.137.–	DM 162,–	£ 55.00
☐ ART FOR SURVIVAL: THE ILLUSTRATOR AND THE ENVIRONMENT	SFR. 79.–	DM 89,–	£ 35.00

(FOR ORDERS FROM EC COUNTRIES V.A.T. WILL BE CHARGED
IN ADDITION TO ABOVE BOOK PRICES)

FOR CREDIT CARD PAYMENT (DEBITED IN SWISS FRANCS):
☐ AMERICAN EXPRESS   ☐ DINER'S CLUB
☐ VISA/BARCLAYCARD/CARTE BLEUE

CARD NO.   EXP. DATE

CARDHOLDER NAME

SIGNATURE

☐ PLEASE BILL ME (ADDITIONAL MAILING COSTS WILL BE
  CHARGED)

(PLEASE PRINT)

LAST NAME   FIRST NAME

TITLE

COMPANY

ADDRESS

CITY   POSTAL CODE

COUNTRY

PLEASE SEND ORDER FORM TO:
GRAPHIS PRESS CORP.
DUFOURSTRASSE 107
CH–8008 ZÜRICH, SWITZERLAND

REQUEST FOR CALL FOR ENTRIES
PLEASE PUT ME ON YOUR "CALL FOR ENTRIES" LIST FOR THE
FOLLOWING TITLES:

☐ GRAPHIS DESIGN   ☐ GRAPHIS ANNUAL REPORTS
☐ GRAPHIS DIAGRAM   ☐ GRAPHIS CORPORATE IDENTITY
☐ GRAPHIS POSTER   ☐ GRAPHIS PACKAGING
☐ GRAPHIS PHOTO   ☐ GRAPHIS LETTERHEAD
☐ GRAPHIS LOGO   ☐ GRAPHIS TYPOGRAPHY

SUBMITTING MATERIAL TO ANY OF THE ABOVE TITLES QUALIFIES
SENDER FOR A DISCOUNT TOWARDS PURCHASE OF THAT TITLE.

G R A P H I S   M A G A Z I N E

MAGAZINE	USA	CANADA	SOUTHAMERICA/ ASIA/PACIFIC
☐ ONE YEAR (6 ISSUES)	US$ 89.00	US$ 99.00	US$ 125.00
☐ TWO YEARS (12 ISSUES)	US$ 159.00	US$ 179.00	US$ 235.00

☐ 25% DISCOUNT FOR STUDENTS WITH COPY OF VALID,
DATED STUDENT ID AND PAYMENT WITH ORDER

☐ CHECK ENCLOSED

USE CREDIT CARDS (DEBITED IN US DOLLARS)

☐ AMERICAN EXPRESS

☐ MASTERCARD

☐ VISA

CARD NO. _____ EXP. DATE _____

CARDHOLDER NAME _____

SIGNATURE _____

☐ PLEASE BILL ME

(PLEASE PRINT)

NAME _____

TITLE _____

COMPANY _____

ADDRESS _____

CITY _____

STATE/PROVINCE _____ ZIP CODE _____

COUNTRY _____

SEND ORDER FORM AND MAKE CHECK PAYABLE TO:
GRAPHIS US, INC.,
141 LEXINGTON AVENUE,
NEW YORK, NY 10016-8193, USA

SERVICE BEGINS WITH ISSUE THAT IS CURRENT WHEN ORDER
IS PROCESSED. (C9B0A)

MAGAZINE	EUROPE/AFRICA MIDDLE EAST	GERMANY	U.K.
☐ ONE YEAR (6 ISSUES)	SFR. 164.–	DM 190,–	£ 68.00
☐ TWO YEARS (12 ISSUES)	SFR. 295.–	DM 342,–	£ 122.00
☐ AIRMAIL SURCHARGES	SFR 65.–	DM 75,–	£ 30.00
☐ REGISTERED MAIL	SFR 20.–	DM 24,–	£ 9.00

☐ CHECK ENCLOSED (PLEASE MAKE SFR.–CHECK PAYABLE TO
A SWISS BANK)

☐ STUDENTS MAY REQUEST A 25% DISCOUNT BY SENDING
STUDENT ID

FOR CREDIT CARD PAYMENT (ALL CARDS DEBITED IN SWISS
FRANCS):

☐ AMERICAN EXPRESS   ☐ DINER'S CLUB

☐ VISA/BARCLAYCARD/CARTE BLEUE

CARD NO. _____ EXP. DATE _____

CARDHOLDER NAME _____

SIGNATURE _____

☐ PLEASE BILL ME

(PLEASE PRINT)

LAST NAME _____

FIRST NAME _____

TITLE _____

COMPANY _____

ADDRESS _____

CITY _____ POSTAL CODE _____

COUNTRY _____

NOTE TO GERMAN SUBSCRIBERS ONLY:
ICH ERKLÄRE MICH EINVERSTANDEN, DASS MEINE NEUE ADRESSE
DURCH DIE POST AN DEN VERTRIEB WEITERGELEITET WIRD.

PLEASE SEND ORDER FORM AND MAKE CHECK PAYABLE TO:
GRAPHIS PRESS CORP.
DUFOURSTRASSE 107
CH–8008 ZÜRICH, SWITZERLAND

SERVICE BEGINS WITH ISSUE THAT IS CURRENT WHEN ORDER
IS PROCESSED. (C9B0A)